Dedicated to all who had the vision and
took the risks over 50 years to make
Port Canaveral the success it is today.

Malcolm E. McLouth 1/21/05

Staying *the* Course

Port Canaveral — The First 50 Years

Aerial view of the harbor inlet on Dedication Day, November 4, 1953

Produced for Canaveral Port Authority by Wolf Jessee Paquin Communications

Researcher/Author: Rachel Moehle
Editor in Chief: Dixie Sansom, Canaveral Port Authority
Editor: Rosalind Postell, Canaveral Port Authority
Photographs: Canaveral Port Authority, John D' Albora, Malcolm "Mac" McLouth, and Roger Wolf
Noah Butt Speech: Courtesy of Noah Butt, Jr.

Partners in Progress:
Pages 76 through 93 profile some of the key firms that were instrumental in the
development and progress of the Port and who helped make this book possible:
Carnival Cruise Lines, FLORIDA TODAY, Gee & Jenson/CH2M HILL, Hoyman Dobson
& Company, P.A., Mid-Florida Freezer Warehouses, Ltd., and Olsen Associates, Inc.

Publisher:

Wolf Jessee Paquin Communications
Cocoa, Florida
Roger Wolf, *President & Chief Executive Officer*
Raymond Jessee, *Vice President & Senior Art Director*
Jonathan Bowering, *Senior Designer*

ISBN Number: 0-9746677-0-6

Library of Congress Control Number: 2003114330

©2003 Wolf Jessee Paquin Communications

JEB BUSH
GOVERNOR OF THE STATE OF FLORIDA

October 31, 2003

Dear Friends:

It is a pleasure to extend congratulations to Port Canaveral on celebrating 50 years of "Bringing the World to You." Milestones such as this provide a special source of encouragement.

I understand since its inception and construction, the Port has become a hub of activity, serving as one of the world's premier cruise destinations and importing and exporting valuable goods. I commend Port Canaveral for being the first quadra modal port in the world, interchanging cargo among sea, land, air and space. The outstanding efforts of Port-related businesses help employ some 30,000 residents throughout Central Florida with an economic benefit of $808 million. I applaud the primary goal of the Canaveral Port Authority to provide a stable and growing employment base for area residents.

Congratulations on 50 years of service and best wishes for continued success.

Sincerely,

Jeb Bush

Jeb Bush

JB/ham

INTRODUCTION

It is my honor to serve as the chairman of the Canaveral Port Authority as we celebrate our first half-century and plan for the future of the Port. Fifty years ago, on November 4, 1953, the Port was dedicated by one of the finest statesmen our state has ever had, the late U.S. Senator Spessard Holland. The mission of the Canaveral Port Authority always has been to strengthen the economy of Brevard County and the Central Florida region by developing trade and creating jobs. From the visionary leadership of those Brevard and Central Florida pioneers who understood the potential value of establishing an outlet to the sea, Port Canaveral has developed from a small oil and shrimp port into the world's second busiest cruise port and a hub for international cargo.

In addition to welcoming more than two million cruise passengers each year, there are more recreational opportunities at Port Canaveral than at all the other thirteen Florida deepwater ports combined. Visitors can enjoy harbor-front dining at one of several restaurants, as well as swimming, fishing, and boating.

Another great benefit to the Central Florida community is Foreign Trade Zone 136 at Port Canaveral. It allows businesses to reduce or eliminate taxes on merchandise stored in warehouses located in the zone. Port Canaveral is the world's only quadramodal port, with cargo links via sea, land, air, and space.

Having spent millions in improvements during the past fifty years, more acres of waterfront land still are available to be developed. Our efforts have focused on expanding and diversifying the cargo base; upgrading facilities; meeting new security mandates; and ensuring highway connectors remain uncongested.

It has taken many years of partnering with area community, business, civic, and elected leaders from Brevard County, the Orlando area, and throughout all of Central Florida to implement the vision of Port Canaveral. During the next fifty years, we will build upon that vision and continue our efforts to maintain Port Canaveral as "Central Florida's outlet to the sea."

Thank you for your support, and we look forward to having you visit our fine gem in the near future.

Sincerely,

Rodney S Ketcham

Rodney S. Ketcham, Chairman
Canaveral Port Authority

TABLE OF CONTENTS

Mr. Chairman, Distinguished Guests, Ladies and Gentlemen:

Port Dedication Speech: The Honorable Noah B. Butt

This day marks the fulfillment of a dream of virtually a century, by dedicating this port to the use of the public. I am, therefore, happy to see so many of you who reside throughout the whole of Brevard County and Central Florida, to be here to join with us in a spirit of rejoicing and of thanksgiving.

I now wish to call to your attention one significant fact, which statement will be in part the language of another, "At last, it's up there, Old Glory."

If I may digress, I wish to call to your attention some important facts with respect to this port. The Plan upon which it was constructed, as you see it today, was conceived through the inspiration of one Mr. Tom Monahan of Indianapolis, Indiana. Afterwards, Mr. Monahan employed the late Colonel C. C. Kirkpatrick and his assistant, Mr. Julian Langner, who is with us today, to make an industrial survey of the port area for the purpose of gathering factual information to submit to the Corps of United States Engineers, in order to establish the economic justification of the Government expending public funds in the development of this enterprise. Upon the plan presented by Mr. Monahan and the industrial survey made by Colonel Kirkpatrick, the 77th Congress of the United States adopted Public Document Number 367, authorizing the construction of the port and the expenditure of government funds, provided local interests met the requirements stated in such document. This local interests did.

> I now wish to call to your attention one significant fact, which statement will be in part the language of another, "At last, it's up there, Old Glory."
>
> – Noah B. Butt

TRANSPLAN
PIPE AND
K POLYETH
N MULCH
FOR TWO

In the meantime, an Act was passed at the 1939 session of the Florida legislature which made this port possible.

Now, this port, like the City of Rome, was not constructed in one day. It has taken years of toil and study in order to construct it. Therefore, I consider it most befitting to mention the names of those, in addition to the present members of the Port Authority, who have contributed their time and their talents toward making it a reality. And in doing so, I mention the name of the late A. Fortenberry, to whose memory this flagpole, which was so generously donated to the Port Authority through the generosity of the Florida Power and Light Company, is now dedicated.

Also, the names of Dr. Bob Schlernitzauer, who was the first chairman of the Authority, and William G. Akridge, who was the first vice-chairman; the late Ward C. Klingensmith, of Titusville; the late John A. Witter, the grand old man of Cocoa Beach; Robert L. Geiger, better known as "Uncle Bob Geiger", that most beloved man of Rockledge; Samuel L. Knutsen, W. B. Lewis and M. N. Argabrite, who is now serving in the capacity of executive secretary of the Port Authority, and whose duties cannot be duplicated.

I wish also to mention the names of men who held offices of trust, which include former United States Senator Claude Pepper, who played a wonderful part in bringing the port up to the proportions by which you view it today. Also, our former Congressman, Joe Hendrix. And, in addition thereto, our thanks and respects go out, not only to your guest speaker, but to Congressman Syd Herlong and Senator George Smathers, who are this day serving us.

And, we must not and shall not forget to mention the name of our late United States Senator Charles O. Andrews, whose services were so invaluable during the critical and promotional states of this enterprise.

I am extremely happy to announce to you that it is with pleasure that we see our own editor, Mrs. Marie Holderman, editor and publisher of The Cocoa Tribune, with us today. And, also Mr. H. H. Hudson of Titusville, publisher and editor of the Titusville Star Advocate. Each of these persons has carried the flagstaff of Port Canaveral throughout the circulation area of their respective papers.

And, also, I am most happy to see the representatives of the ORLANDO MORNING SENTINEL and the ORLANDO EVENING STAR, publications which have been the standard bearers of Port Canaveral throughout the whole of Central Florida.

By dedicating Port Canaveral today, to the use of the public, it will open the gateway into the whole of Central Florida, for the reception of ship-laden cargo to be distributed throughout that area. The progressive and enterprising city of Orlando, which is only a few miles to the west of us, the hub city of Central Florida, having a distributive area covering in whole or in part 13 counties right in the heart of Florida, which area has a population equal to one-fourth the population of the entire state of Florida, will be one of the largest, if not the largest user of this Port.

United States Senator

Spessard Holland made

the principal address,

calling it "Our nation's

port for inner and

outer space."

When it comes to our guest speaker, it is not necessary for me or any other man in Central Florida to introduce him to you for the reason that I feel assured that by far the greater percentage of you could have recognized him by sight and called him by name. There is no yardstick, known to me, by which the services he has rendered in developing this port to the proportions whereby it can be opened for the purpose of receiving ocean-borne commerce for distribution throughout this area can be measured.

In 1939, while then a State Senator, he voted for the bill that made this port possible. Later, as Governor of the State of Florida, he gave to the Late Colonel C. C. Kirkpatrick his strong official endorsement of Port Canaveral, copies of which were transmitted to the Corps of United States Engineers along with the Kirkpatrick report; and since he has been your United States Senator, he has untiringly and unceasingly offered every aid and assistance which is humanly possible for a man to do towards the development of Port Canaveral.

Therefore, I consider it a single honor to me to have the privilege of introducing to you my friend and your friend, Florida's senior United States Senator, the Honorable Spessard L. Holland.

Photo right: Dedication Day, November 4, 1953

PORT CANAVERAL'S FIRST DECADE

Canaveral Port Authority's

first official meeting place,

where all the dreams

were conceived.

I t was the culmination of a long-awaited dream and a cause for great celebration when, on November 4, 1953, Port Canaveral officially was dedicated. Flags were flying and bands playing. Five thousand pounds of fried mullet, 300 pounds of baked beans, 500 gallons of cole slaw and 20 gallons of pickles were consumed. United States Senator Spessard Holland made the principal address, calling it "Our nation's port for inner and outer space." Later, as darkness fell, the festivities moved inland with two formal balls held at the Indian River Hotel in Rockledge and the American Legion Hall in Cocoa.

Cape Canaveral has been significant historically for centuries, as it is the oldest geographical name still in use in the Western Hemisphere. It was in 1520 that Spanish ship Captain Francisco Gordillo sent a small party of men ashore. They were attacked by Indians using arrows made of the cane growing there, inspiring Gordillo to name the place Capo de Canaveral, Place of the Cane Bearers.

More than 300 years later, in 1878, the Department of the Navy asked Congress to create a deepwater port at Canaveral, but the proposal was rejected because it had little economic value. Six more attempts were made throughout the years to get the harbor dug, but it was not until 1929 that the United States Engineers Office in Jacksonville found justification for the project and approved it.

Photo right: In 1953 commercial fishing
began at Port Canaveral.

> It was only "a hole in a muddy channel with a tiny warehouse and some fishing boats on the north side."
>
> – *Florida Today special section saluting the Port's 25th anniversary.*

The original charter in 1939 established a seven-member board of port commissioners but it was not until 1941 that the Port Authority was authorized to advertise the levying of a tax with a three mill cap within the Port District, which consisted of an area bounded in the south by present-day Pineda Causeway and in the north by the southern boundary of the City of Titusville. In 1945, Congress approved the construction as part of the Rivers and Harbors Improvement Program

and, a year later, appropriated $830,000 for construction with the proviso the amount be matched through "local interest."

Voters Say "Yes!" to Canaveral Harbor

Selling the idea of a port was not an easy task, but many community leaders with vision worked hard to make it a reality. Fishermen especially were eager to see it happen and worked hard to get it approved because it would be such a quick outlet to the ocean. The closest other inlets were Ft. Pierce and Mayport (Jacksonville).

In November 1947, freeholders of the Port District went to the polls and overwhelmingly approved a bond issue that would pave the way for the digging of Port Canaveral. There had been rumors circulating that opponents of the Port would attempt to keep voters away from the polls, so J. J. Jackson, attorney for the Port Authority, enlisted the aid of his son, Edward, (who succeeded his father as Port counsel in 1971) and some of his friends on the Cocoa High School football team. They made themselves available to escort hesitant voters from their cars to the polling places so they could cast their ballots without incident.

On December 1 of that year, the Port Authority issued $1,365,999 in bonds for construction of the harbor, channel and Barge Canal; and on June 6, 1950, a dredge started cutting a path east from the middle of the Indian River to the Port site. Most of the dredge spoil was used later to construct the Bennett Causeway that linked the Port and beaches to the Central

Florida area, but some of it wound up creating landfill for many of the buildings which occupy the Banana River shoreline in Cape Canaveral.

Roger Dobson, former county commissioner, who was born on the Cape and who grew up in a commercial fishing family, was away at college during the digging of the Port, but he remembers a harrowing experience on one of his vacations at home. While duck hunting one morning, he waded out in the Banana River and found himself slowly sinking into the mud. Known as "blue mud" to the locals, this was a layer of deep spoil deposited on top of the fine sand the dredges had first turned up. "It was a scary thing," he said. "It was like quicksand and I had no way of knowing how deep it was. And I guess my boots are still out there to this day."

In October 1951, a bulldozer cut through from the harbor to the sea and the waters of the Atlantic Ocean began to merge with those of the Banana River as the tides finished the job. Commercial fishermen began to use the new deepwater Port immediately and were delighted to be able to harvest cold water tuna and swordfish for the first time.

Sara Nisbet, widow of Port Commissioner David Nisbet, remembers that the first bridge across the Barge Canal on North Courtenay Parkway was not a bridge at all. "It actually was a barge," she says, "anchored in place at each end so it could be moved aside if boats needed to come through. The banks of the new canal were sloped so that cars could drive down to the water level and cross on the barge to the other side, but it was a bit precarious and school bus drivers wouldn't even attempt it." In fact, school buses drove the children who lived north of the canal on Merritt Island to Titusville and back down to Cocoa until the barge was replaced with a real bridge in the 1960s. Trucks hauling fruit from the citrus growers north of the canal suffered a similar inconvenience because it was impossible for them to navigate the barge crossing.

The Port Begins to Grow

The first employee of the Port was Barbara Smith, who celebrated her 50th anniversary of employment in 2001; and the first revenue received by Port Canaveral was a check for $4,000 from Joseph Luley, president of the Canaveral Corporation. Chairman Noah B. Butt accepted it in 1951 as payment on the first annual "readiness to serve" charge made by the Port Authority. An agreement with Luley provided for construction of an oil tank farm adjacent to the Port and the laying of a pipeline from the farm to the 400-foot marginal wharf that would be completed two years later.

The first employee of the Port was Barbara Smith, who celebrated her 50th anniversary of employment in 2001.

Money was tight in the early days of Port Canaveral, with most funding coming from taxes levied. In 1941, the operating budget was $7,494.12, all of which came from a tax levy of one mill. By its dedication year, the budget had grown to $53,500, with a tax levy of three mills producing $38,000. Only $15,500 came from operating income, primarily from tenants. By 1956, the budget had grown to $64,818 with $20,000 from earned income.

Dedication Day, November 4, 1953, was a fabulous celebration at the Port and provided great excitement for attendees.

Noah B. Butt, Jr. remembers that once during the Port's early operation, his father, Chairman Butt, and Port Commissioner Nisbet had to go to the bank to guarantee personally the payroll checks because there was so little money in the operating account. "My dad was often called 'Mr. Canaveral'," said Butt, "and he would be amazed if he could see it today. It is bigger and better than he ever could have imagined."

Dobson had a chance to overwhelm his grandfather, one of the early

Photo left: USS McClelland (PE 750) was moored at the west marginal wharf for an open house.

lighthouse keepers at Cape Canaveral, with a sight of the Port shortly after it was opened. He picked him up at a nursing home and drove him to the edge of the harbor on what is now North Atlantic Avenue in Cape Canaveral. "When he saw it," said Dobson, "he was speechless. He kept saying over and over, 'I don't believe it; I just don't believe it finally has happened.' "

In February 1952, the construction of a 400-foot fishing dock was approved but before it was finished, it was ordered extended another 200 feet. Dock space was leased to Hudgins Fish Company, Fischers' Seafood, Cook and Lewis, S. Salvador and Sons, the Cove Fish Market, and Bennett's Seafood Market, which also was granted a license to sell fishing supplies, bait and tackle, and food. Leases cost $1,200 per year. That same year Thomas R. Stuart was appointed the Port's first harbormaster and pilot.

A New Port Governance Structure Ushers in a New Era of Growth

In 1953, the governance structure of the Port changed. The seven-member board authorized by the original charter had consisted of county commissioners from districts one, two and five; the mayors of the City of Cocoa and the City of Rockledge; and elected representatives from precincts 12 and 22. Nisbet, who had won his county commission seat on a write-in ballot, realized that the system of governance was making the Port a political football, so he became the driving force in getting the system changed. The new charter provided for five separate Port districts with an

elected commissioner from each. The first five to serve under the new rule were Butt, Nisbet, L. M. Carpenter, A. A. Dunn and G. W. Laycock.

The five new commissioners authorized jetty construction immediately with a Congressional appropriation of $610,000, and in 1955, the new harbor got its first visit from a cargo ship. The S/S Mormac Spruce, under charter to Military Sealift Command, docked at the Marginal Wharf and loaded cargo from Patrick Air Force Base destined for St. Lucia in the British West Indies.

By 1955, Fruit Industries, Inc. had a processing plant and cold storage tanks with a one million gallon capacity at the Port. The Cocoa Tribune held the presses for its August 26th issue in order to print news of the lease-signing for the $2 million dollar plant. "The way we feel about it," wrote Managing

Photo above: Seated are N.M. Agrabite, Executive Treasurer; Chairman N.B. Butt, Secretary Barbara Smith. Standing left to right are Vice Chairman A.A. Dunn, and Commissioners G.W. Laycock, Dave S. Nisbet, and L.M. Carpenter.

Editor John Pound, "no news of such importance has been printed in this paper in a long time."

Juice was hydraulically pumped through underground stainless steel pipes directly to the *S/S Tropicana* for shipment to New York, where it was pumped out and packaged for distribution. In 1958, however, the *Tropicana* hit and severely damaged the west marginal wharf, which was under repair for twenty-two months. The repairs, first attempted by an engineering firm hired by the ship's owners, proved unsatisfactory and the Port filed a lawsuit for damages. Young Edward Jackson, new to his father's law firm, helped prosecute the suit for the Port, and he remembers the 1961 trial well. "It resulted in the largest jury award ever made in Brevard County at that time," he said, "and I knew things were going our way when the foreman of the jury came out and asked for an adding machine."

In addition to the Tropicana tanks, Mid-Florida Oil Company also had underground tanks which stored six million gallons of the type of oil used in industrial boilers and power plants. It was brought to the Port by tankers and trucked to Vero Beach, Orlando and Daytona Beach.

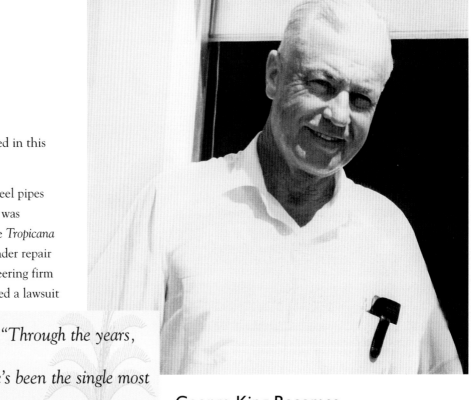

"Through the years, he's been the single most important part of the Port. He's been the 'King of the Port' and always will be."

– *Port Authority Chairman Malcolm "Mac" McLouth*

George King Becomes the First Port Manager

It also was in 1954 that the Port took a giant leap forward with the hiring of its first professional manager, George King. He would serve in that position for nearly a quarter of a century, retiring in 1977. At his retirement party, then Port Authority Chairman Malcolm "Mac" McLouth, saluted him. "George is a person who always gave so much of himself to his job," he said. "Through the years, he's been the single most important part of the Port. He's been the 'King of the Port' and always will be."

Photo above: George King
Photo left: The S/S Tropicana carried citrus juice to New York

VACATION AT COCOA—Excellent Accommodations, Swimming, Fishing, Boating, Golf
LIVE IN COCOA—MODERN SCHOOLS, CHURCHES, HOSPITAL, RECREATION, CONVENIENT SHOPPING

Advertisements like the one

above were used to attract

visitors to the Port Canaveral

area. The Cape Canaveral

Launch Area continues

to be an important part

of the space program.

1957 and 1958 saw big plans for new growth at the Port. A resolution was passed and lobbying began at the Federal level for the Canaveral Lock, so necessary if the harbor was to serve industry throughout the entire Port taxing district and materially benefit the entire county. The state legislature was asked to approve construction of the new Bennett Causeway (State Road 528). Property was sold to the United States Air Force on the north side of the Port for $710,000, and the first cargo shipment of steel arrived on the MS *Anvers* — 800 tons of it to be used in the construction of guided missile assembly plants at the Cape Canaveral Launch Area. A fuel and ice dock was created and a 100-foot addition to the warehouse on the south side was completed.

In the remaining years of its first decade, the Port entered into an accelerated period of expansion. The program for 1959-60 included plans for an office building onsite for the Port Authority, a petroleum unloading facility, more warehouse facilities and a 200-foot extension to the wharf, for a total financial commitment of $500,000. Ad valorem taxes were set for only one mill and the budget had grown to $205,700, with nearly one-third of it from operating income. Port Canaveral was moving steadily away from taxation and toward financial independence. It also was in 1960 that the Port played its first role in the nation's defense program with the firing of two Polaris missiles from thirty miles offshore, heading on a course down range. It was the first of many such firings in the development of the guided missile program, including the Polaris, Poseidon and Trident missiles.

1961 was an important year in the progress of the growing harbor. Port Canaveral became a port of entry in April and no longer was dependent on Customs and Immigration services from the Port of Palm Beach or Miami. During that year, land was leased to the United States Coast Guard for a sea/air rescue station. In June 1961, the first meeting of the Port Authority was held on site at the new administration building. It had been built at a cost of $31,728, with an additional $7,519 spent for paving, grading and planting grass.

The following year, the sand transfer plant at the north jetty was authorized by the Federal Rivers and Harbors Act of October 23, 1962. Port commissioners, realizing that the sand transfer plant would be an essential part of maintaining the entrance channel and preserving the beaches south of the jetties, had worked hard to get this legislation through Congress. Unfortunately, it still would be more than a decade before it would be operational.

And that same year, longtime Port Commissioner W.O.B. Chittenden resigned due to ill health. In his letter of resignation, he wrote, "It is my opinion that this East Coast Port will someday be one of the nation's most important." If he were alive today, he would be amazed to know just how accurate that prediction would prove to be.

Photo: Lumber was one of the first cargo industries at the Port.

PORT CANAVERAL: "THE SLEEPING GIANT" SAILS INTO ITS SECOND DECADE

Dignitaries cut the ribbon for the grand opening of the Canaveral Lock

It was a bright sunny day in 1965 when dignitaries on the first vessel cut the ribbon at the Canaveral Lock, signaling another major milestone for the growing Port. Port Commissioner John D'Albora chaired the ceremonial event that marked the occasion. His father's boat, with special guest United States Senator Spessard Holland aboard, was the first vessel to navigate the waters from the Banana River channel to the ocean. After the ceremonies, the Port Authority Commissioners and guests boarded a bus to the Cape to view the successful launch of an unmanned rocket.

At the end of the first year, 1,470 boats, 5,992 passengers, eighty-one towboats and 113 barges had traveled through the Lock.

The Port began the decade with a budget of $336,000, with about a third of it coming from earned income and the rest from taxation. By the end of 1967, revenue had jumped to $272,828 with a prediction of $450,000 for 1968. The number of ships docking had increased from sixty-two to 125 with 200 predicted for the next year. Cargo had increased from 342,000 tons to 1,526,992 tons, with a prediction of 2,000,000 tons for 1968.

Photo right: A large crowd gathered for the ribbon cutting ceremony of the Canaveral Lock.

The "Sleeping Giant" Pushes Forward

Called "the sleeping giant" by the *Orlando Sentinel*, the Port began to push marketing opportunities with a portable exhibit and attendance at industrial expos in Orlando and throughout the state. Ads were placed in conjunction with the Brevard Economic Development Council in trade publications and newspapers.

While cargo continued to be the primary thrust in marketing efforts, it was in 1967 that new Commissioner Malcolm "Mac" McLouth proposed that the authority make a pitch to Central Florida's brand new Walt Disney World as its "outlet to the sea" for both goods and people. That year, Holland America's *S/S Rotterdam* had docked to embark passengers for a chartered cruise. The first cruise ship to sail from the Port had been four years earlier when the *S/S Yarmouth* boarded 402 passengers for a sold-out cruise to Nassau over Labor Day weekend 1963. Even though regular cruises operating from the Port were only a dream for the distant future, in 1972 the Authority authorized the construction of a freight/passenger terminal. With marketing-minded McLouth leading the way, they said "We must let the industry know we are interested in cruise business."

McLouth Leads the Port in New Directions

McLouth, now Executive Director of the Port, has spent more than half his life helping develop Port Canaveral. He was the first Republican elected to the Port Authority and he brought a new perspective to the Board.

His first encounter with the Port was in 1966, while he was serving as a Boy Scout leader. He went on a weekend camping trip with his troupe to Jetty Park, which had recently opened. "We pitched our pup tents," he said, "and I remember being so impressed with the beauty and serenity of the place. Being an engineer and working as I did in growth and development, I thought it would be wonderful if we could find a way to ensure that this place could escape development and always be kept as a park for people to use."

A couple of months later he was involved in politics and was looking for people from his party to run for office in the county, "no mean feat," he said, "for a Republican back then." He couldn't find anybody to run for Port Commissioner, so, remembering that Jetty Park weekend, he decided to do it himself. At first, he said, he thought he'd just file to run for the post and sit back and see what happened. But then he began to go to the Port Authority meetings prior to the election and saw the potential there. "I got hooked on the place," he said, "so I campaigned hard because I wanted to get on that Board and make a difference."

George King was a hard man to get to know, McLouth said, "but he won me over and I won him over, and together we began to market the Port. King knew the business inside out and he wanted to see it grow. He had great vision and his philosophy was 'build and they will come'." At that time, McLouth said, the space industry totally overwhelmed the economy of the area, but King saw a similar future for the Port.

Photo: Holland America's S/S Rotterdam

"From the outset, everyone on that Board was dedicated to seeing the Port become self-sufficient," he said, "and politics played little part in it. Once they got accustomed to a Yankee Republican in their midst, I earned their respect and all four Democrats actually elected me Chairman for three consecutive terms, beginning in 1977."

Environment and Recreation Enter the Picture

Jetty Park, which first inspired McLouth, continued to grow. By July 1969, it had 140 campsites with water and electrical hook-ups, tables and grills. An aerial photo of the park was included in the May 1969 issue of *Trailer Life* magazine.

The environment became a concern as early as 1968 when the Port Authority authorized a study and follow-up report on water pollution potential at the Port, with recommendations to prevent fouling of water abutting Port land. The comprehensive report included investigations of possible cost sharing opportunities with the Federal government; future dockside collections; holding and sewage disposal facilities needed; marina and industry water disposal standards; adequacy of existing laws and regulations; water purity monitoring programs; and oil skimming, floating trash removal needs.

Two years later another study was authorized of the Port's ability to control a major ship fire, which led eventually to a fire protection agreement with the City of Cape Canaveral — the beginning of a long and mutually beneficial relationship between the two entities.

Photo: Aerial view of Jetty Park.

"It would be wonderful if we could find a way to ensure that this place could escape development and always be kept as a park for people to use."

– Malcolm "Mac" McLouth

Newsprint cargo volume and tornado damage necessitated construction of new warehouses.

Increased Cargo Creates Demand for New Facilities

Facilities were expanded during the decade to meet the demands of a burgeoning cargo industry. Newsprint had become a major import and the Port was fast running out of space to store it. In addition, in April 1966, a tornado had severely damaged a warehouse and some of the newsprint stored there. So Manager King was authorized to prepare specifications for a new warehouse, which was built for a cost of $245,594.

Long-Range Plan for Growth is Commissioned

It was also in 1966 that the Commissioners realized the need for long-range planning and commissioned the Frederic R. Harris Company of New York to develop a long-range economic study for Port Canaveral. The comprehensive study ran to more than one hundred pages and examined the economic base of Central Florida as well as the competition posed by other Florida Ports.

The report noted that the twenty-five ports in Florida represented an important industry, following tourism, agriculture and manufacturing, as one of the ranking job providers in the state. It went on to say, "Port Canaveral itself will handle increasing volumes of commerce, primarily receipts, but with increased possibilities for coastal and foreign shipments as the general economy of the tributary area grows."

Photo right: Continental Cement silos and tanker berths on the south side of the Port

The United States Navy uses the Trident turning basin for all its water operations at the Port.

Recommendations for commodities deserving of continued marketing emphasis were petroleum products, cement and masonry, citrus, newsprint and steel. Waterfront utilization was termed a "knotty" problem. "The Port has a limited amount of water frontage within which the commission must endeavor to accommodate many requests," the report stated. "Simultaneously, the commission also must continue to concern itself with the necessity for preserving Port land for future essential installations as well as for waterborne-commerce oriented industries. . . [therefore] it is recommended that the master development plans indicate only certain waterfront areas for non-deepwater usage on short term bases.

"This course of action will have the desired effect of preserving access for bona fide deepwater users, until such time as volume and economic feasibility dictate development of the north side of the channel for Port use."

Coast Guard Sets Up Station at Port

A lease was approved in January 1963 with the United States Coast Guard, and the first vessel, the Cutter *Courageous*, arrived in September 1971. The welcoming committee included Admiral O. R. Smeder, Commander of the Seventh Coast Guard District. The Port Authority, in a gesture of welcome, had the ship's bell engraved marking the occasion.

Photo: Trident turning basin and pier under construction.

Captain Thomas Stuart, the Port's first harbormaster and chief pilot, died in February 1967 and Captain Fred Degendorf was appointed to the position. In 1969 the Authority began taking steps to have the harbor deepened to forty feet and to extend the channel westward with the construction of a second turning basin.

A major event occurred in September 1972 when Ray Industries sought to purchase land on the barge canal for Sea Ray Boats. The company planned a $2 million investment and the Port's attorney, Ed Jackson, was asked to get the Port's land appraised. A small group of people, opposed to the Port's expansion, managed to get the County Prosecuting Attorney to file

Sunshine Law violations against three commissioners and Jackson because they refused to identify the name of the appraiser. The four men were indicted by a grand jury, but the presiding judge in the case, after reviewing the facts, dismissed the charges as frivolous.

Jackson had only recently become the Port's attorney, taking over the duties from his father, J. J. Jackson. "When this thing happened," says the younger Jackson (now a retired judge), "my dad said, 'Well, son, you've only been their attorney for a year and you've managed to get most of them indicted'."

Photo above: Left to right (back row): Commissioner Roderick McIver, Port Manager George King,
Commissioner Robert Cutter and Attorney J.J. Jackson;
(front row) Commissioners Kelly Brinson, Chairman Arthur Dunn and John D'Albora

In a more serious vein, Jackson continued, "The Port has been fortunate to have good, honest businessmen guiding it through all of its 50 years, and it also has been fortunate to have a legislative delegation that has been very supportive of its needs."

Jane Clendinen Roberts, daughter of Port Commissioner James Clendinen, echoes Jackson's statement. "My Dad always said political differences were put aside by the Commissioners because they were so dedicated to the Port and motivated by its needs." She has memories of Sunshine Law problems herself when, on one occasion, several of the Commissioners were criticized for getting together for a picnic lunch on the breaker walls prior to a meeting. "My dad was furious at the pettiness" she says, "so he painted a big, orange sun on the side of an old-fashioned lunch pail and took that and his fishing pole out to the jetties for the next lunch gathering. That way he could say he was always operating in the sunshine."

The Port Continues to Move Forward

With legal difficulties over, Ray Industries made their land purchase and brought major economic growth to the Port and to Brevard County. The operating budget continued to grow and the gap between income from taxation and operating income continued to close. At the end of its first twenty years, the "Sleeping Giant" was about to rise and shine.

Photo left: Development of southwest end of the Port harbor

A GROWING PORT FOR A GROWTH MARKET — THE THIRD DECADE

Great changes were ahead for Port Canaveral as it entered its third decade. The operating budget reached $1 million for the first time in 1973 and income from revenue was $400,000, nearly approaching the equal mark with tax revenue. The next year, 1974, the budget was supported by a tax levy of only .666 mills, the first time it had been under one mill. In 1977, with a levy of .6 mills, earned income exceeded tax dollars for the first time. The operating budget was $1,359,128, with $700,000 of it coming from fees and rentals.

By 1973, the Port had received $2.7 million in grants for improvements on the south side and the Federal Economic Development Administration granted another $1,363,500 for more construction. A loading dock for fresh citrus was completed in November 1975, in hopes of reaching a long-standing goal of exporting Indian River citrus to markets in Europe and Japan. In 1978 that dream came true. That year 732,141 cartons of citrus and 267,869 cartons of produce were loaded into eleven ships bound for Europe and two for Japan.

Commissioner Dave Nisbet was quoted in the Vero Beach *Press Journal*, saying: "Port Canaveral is a natural point for citrus exports from this area because of its convenient, centralized and close-by location to so many producers. The Port Authority has taken several

Ribbon cutting for

a new wing of the Port

Authority office

Photo above: (left to right): Commissioners W. O. B. Clendinen, R. A. Cutter, D. A. "Dave" Nisbet; Executive Secretary Barbara Smith; Executive Director Charles "Chuck" Rowland; and Commissioner M. M. "Buck" Buchanan.
Right: Billboard advertising growth opportunities at the Port.

The USS Redstone, like the USS Vanguard were used by NASA as tracking ships.

positive steps to accommodate the citrus trade, including constructing additional truck offloading ramps, providing for the required ventilation and inset protection, and offering facilities separate from other cargo operations. The Port now has over 90,000 square feet to ensure adequate warehouse space in light of increasing demands by other cargoes."

In the summer of 1976, three 400-foot piers were completed on the north side of the Port and the *USS Vangaurd*, a NASA-sponsored tracking ship, docked for one year at the north-south pier while the scrap yard was stabilized on the north side.

Administrative Changes Mark the Third Decade

Other changes were taking place rapidly at the Port in addition to cargo growth. June 1977 saw the establishment of a parking fee of twenty-five cents at Jetty Park and in August, twenty-five new campsites were added to the facility. That same month, retired Navy Captain Glen Cheek was hired as the Port's first assistant manager. He served in this position for only four months, succeeding George King as manager upon King's retirement in December 1977.

There was a big retirement party for the "King of the Port," with all the Commissioners paying him tribute. "George has seen more changes at the Port than will probably ever occur there again," said Port attorney Ed Jackson. "George came onboard when the Port was

nothing but a muddy, freshly dug harbor, and I only hope we don't lose his expertise entirely during his retirement years." Culminating the round of tributes, Chairman Malcolm "Mac" McLouth announced that Port Road was being changed to George King Boulevard in his honor.

Cheek, in reminiscing about those years, said, "Our main thrust was building the cargo business. Passenger business was thought of as 'icing on the cake'. I still remember my first days and weeks at the Port. Barbara Smith had made the Port her life, and she saved me many times with her knowledge and corporate memory. She guarded the Port's business operation very, very carefully."

As the Port's 25th anniversary approached, the pace of business quickened. A new marketing slogan was adopted in 1978: "A growing Port for a growth market — Port Canaveral, the entrance to Central Florida." A six-year timetable for major improvements was adopted. In addition, $185,000 was appropriated for new roads and another $500,000 for another new warehouse to be completed by 1982.

25th Anniversary is a Cause for Celebration

When the time came to celebrate the first twenty-five years in October 1978, the new warehouse was not ready, so a gala cocktail party for 250 people was held in the Southwest corner of the old warehouse. *Florida Today* printed a special section devoted to the Port's history and noted that the food was a bit more glitzy than dedication day in 1953, when the fare was fried mullet, baked beans and cole slaw. This time around, the fishermen and the local restaurants came through with shrimp, crabmeat and other seafood delicacies, as was befitting a booming and bustling Port that was growing rapidly into a major economic force in Central Florida.

During 1979, 172 ships moved through Port Canaveral, carrying 1.5 million tons of fuel oil, 280,000 tons of cement, 53,000 tons of newsprint and 48,000 tons of citrus. It was also in 1979 that the Port finally got the green light from the State Department of Environmental Regulation to dredge the Port's west turning basin, ending nearly two years of delays on the matter. The dredging was essential if the Port was to accommodate the larger tankers and cargo ships.

It was about this same time that the U.S. Navy completed the Trident Submarine Basin at the Port. This project also served as an interim substitute for sand bypassing, as more than 2,800,000 cubic yards of sand, dredged to create the basin, was placed on the beach south of the Port. Bob Kenaston, who was the Lockheed engineer in charge of the project, remembers that he got the shock of his life at the beginning of the project

United States military presence has been an important part of Port Canaveral.

when the Department of the Navy in Washington, D. C. asked him for a project budget. "I hadn't had time to do any detailed cost analysis," he said, "so I just said, 'Oh, it will probably run about 65 million dollars,' and I nearly fell out of my chair when the admiral replied, 'O.K., do it!'."

Madcap Mischief Makers Provide Summer Fun

The summer of 1979 also brought about a little fun and frolic at the Port. The Madcap Mischief Makers (M3) surfaced, planning activities to celebrate the tenth anniversary of NASA's moon landing. Festivities included a sailboat parade, a cocktail party at the north warehouse, the dedication of a monument at Jetty Park commemorating the landing, and a human chain planned to stretch from Jetty Park to South Melbourne Beach. Thousands turned out to form the chain, but, unfortunately, a good many gaps along the way kept it from being continuous.

Hurricane David paid a Labor Day weekend visit to Brevard County in 1979, passing by Port Canaveral about twenty miles at sea during low tide. As water rose nearly to the floors of the warehouses, eleven boats were destroyed in the water and Dick Davis lost all of the docks at his marina. Maximum winds were ninety-five miles per hour but luckily, Port facilities suffered little serious damage.

*Photo far left: George King, "King of the Port",
retired from Port service in 1977
Photo left: A United States
Navy Trident submarine entering the Port.*

"He (Chuck Rowland)

had vision and he was

vital in the expansion of

our cruise industry in

those early days…"

– Malcolm "Mac" McLouth

The West Marginal Wharf did sustain damage in December 1979 when the bulkhead collapsed, putting it out of commission for eighteen months and costing about $2 million to repair. The collapse turned out to be somewhat of a blessing in disguise, however, because the new bulkhead was designed for forty-one feet of water and the platform was redesigned to support greater loads behind the bulkhead.

By March 1980, Cheek had helped bring about a significant increase in business during his two-year tenure as manager. He helped boost annual revenues by $140,000 and oversaw more than $600,000 in capital improvements. Avenue A (Commercial Drive) was renamed in his honor.

Changing the Guard Again: Rowland Takes the Helm

Malcolm "Mac" McLouth was a Port Authority Board member when Charles "Chuck" Rowland took charge. "Chuck brought a different approach to Port management," he said. "He had vision and he was vital in the expansion of our cruise industry in those early days. The success of our cruise industry today is due primarily to him. It's responsible for over seventy percent of our income and is the one thing that made the Port self-sufficient."

"The cruise business was a huge challenge," Rowland remembers. "I thought it would help to have Mickey Mouse come over here to help

us advertise, but Disney was reluctant to have him venture off their property. After all, he was their trademark."

When the *Queen Elizabeth II* made her first visit to Port Canaveral in December 1980, however, Rowland repeated his request for a Disney character to greet the ship. "This time, they were impressed by this distinguished ship choosing to stop at Port Canaveral," he said, "so they sent over Goofy. We took photos, of course, and I asked their people if we could use them in marketing materials."

Again, the answer was "no," but it wasn't long, Rowland said, before Gene LeMoyne, one of the Disney Imagineers, called to make an appointment to discuss some joint marketing ventures. "He came over to meet with me, and the gist of the conversation was that their attendance had suffered during the economic recession of the early 1980s and they were very uneasy about their future, especially since they were in the process of building Epcot. They had come to the conclusion, finally, that there were three reasons visitors came to Florida: Disney, the beaches, and cruises; and since Port Canaveral was the closest port to Walt Disney World and also near a major airport, it would make sense to help develop the cruise trade here. He not only authorized use of the Goofy photos — he wanted to work with the Port to produce a multimedia presentation to take to the cruise lines."

Above: Glen Cheek, Executive Director until 1980
Photos left: Queen Elizabeth II in foreground; USNS Hayes
berthed at North Cargo Pier 3 in background;
Charles M. "Chuck" Rowland, Executive Director

A New Era Begins:
Cruise Ships Begin to Call Canaveral "Home"

Before the presentation was even finished, however, Bruce Nierenberg, CEO of Scandinavian Cruises, contacted Rowland about bringing the *Scandinavian Sea* to the Port for daylong "cruises to nowhere." So Port Canaveral turned 20,000 square feet of the north warehouse into a cruise terminal for about $80,000. "I had a hard time convincing the board to take this plunge," Rowland says. "The vote was three to two."

Cruise Terminal 1 was completed in February 1982. In special ceremonies, it officially was dedicated by Florida's First Lady, Mrs. Bob Graham, and later that same month the *Scandinavian Sea* became the first ship to be homeported at Port Canaveral.

Construction commences on Cruise Terminal 2, the result of Premier Cruise Lines' proposal to bring two new ships to homeport at Port Canaveral.

Later Nierenberg left the Scandinavian line and formed his own company, Premier Cruise Lines, proposing to bring two new ships to homeport at Port Canaveral. This time Rowland had no trouble convincing the board to appropriate funds to build Cruise Terminals 2 and 3; the vote was unanimous. "Chuck's philosophy, like George King's, was 'build them and they will come'," says McLouth. "That doesn't always work, of course, but in that time and this place, it was the right thing to do."

While the cruise business was developing a toe-hold at the Port, cargo was not being neglected. In May 1980, the *Sunbelt Dixie* made her first call at the Port to load citrus — something she would continue to do for the next twenty years. (She was replaced in 2002 by her successor, the *Sunbelt Spirit*.) Later that year, Mid-Florida Freezer made plans to demolish several old buildings and build a new 40,000-square-foot warehouse.

Port Commissioner M. M. "Buck" Buchanan was instrumental in marketing the Port's cargo industry during the early 1980s, traveling all over the world to promote the business. "Cruise ships were the new baby on the horizon," he said, "but cargo was bread and butter. I knew we needed to get this Port expanded beyond shrimping and oil if we were to get it off the tax rolls, which was everybody's goal. So Chuck and I went wherever we could to build up cargo business."

Their efforts were highly successful, for the Port budget exceeded $2 million in 1982 for the first time ever. At the end of its third decade, Port Canaveral was living up to its slogan; it was, indeed, a growing port in a growth market.

Photo: Cruise Terminal 2 under construction

PORT OF CHOICE FOR THE WORLD'S NUMBER ONE TOURIST DESTINATION—THE FOURTH DECADE

Cruise Terminal 4 groundbreaking

The 1980's brought a whole new focus for Port Canaveral: tourism and cruising. Premier Cruise Lines opened the door to this burgeoning new trend in vacationing, completing its corporate headquarters at the Port in October 1983.

Cruise Terminals 2 and 3 were constructed hastily on the Port's south side to accommodate the new ships. The 8,700-square-foot geodesic dome structures were purchased from NASA when their Bicentennial Exhibition closed at the Space Center. There was no furniture, so a deal was made with Eastern Airlines to purchase their old terminal chairs when the Orlando Airport moved from McCoy Air Force Base to its present location.

The terminals, plus piers that were converted from a former tanker berth, a roll-on/roll-off ramp, parking and landscaping, all were completed at a cost of $3.3 million. The terminals were dedicated by Congressman Bill Nelson on May 23, 1983. That same year, ground was broken for Cruise Terminal 4. The ships were getting bigger and the demand for space to berth them was growing at an astronomical pace.

Photo above: Commissioners Thomas L. Newbern, Jerry W. Allender, D. S. "Dave" Nisbet, Malcolm E. McLouth, M. M. "Buck" Buchanan and Executive Director Charles "Chuck" Rowland

Photo right: Cruise Terminal 2

The year 1983 saw a dizzying spurt of growth and change at the Port in many areas. The first Port magazine, *Port Canaveral Capsules*, began publishing that year. At the same time, the new wing at the Port Authority building was opened and dedicated to Barbara Smith, Director of Operations and Administration, in recognition of her long service to the Port. The 2,000 square-foot addition was completed at a cost of $85,546.

In June, the newest Trident submarine arrived at the Port on her maiden voyage. Named the *USS Florida*, she arrived with Governor Bob Graham aboard. In September, a giant tethered balloon was hoisted over the Port. Nicknamed "Fat Albert" by the local populace, its official name was Tethered Aerostat Radar System (TARS). Contrary to popular speculation, its primary use was not drug surveillance but detection and interdiction of unidentified aircraft that might pose a security threat.

In 1985, it broke its tether at Cape Canaveral Air Force Station and drifted away, sinking in the Atlantic. Larger than the Goodyear blimp, Fat Albert was indeed fat, at 175 feet long, fifty-eight feet in diameter and weighing in at 7,700 lbs. It was replaced with a smaller version called a Sea-based Aerostat (SBA), which quickly was dubbed "Fat Albert, Jr."

In March 1984, Premier's *StarShip Royale* was welcomed with a week of special events befitting the Port's first homeported ship for multi-day cruises. There were ceremonies onboard both here and in Nassau as she sailed away on March 26th with 700 passengers. It also was in March that the regal *Queen Elizabeth II* paid her third visit to the Port, docking overnight for the first time.

Earlier that month, tragedy struck when the *Scandinavian Sea* caught on fire at the dock and virtually was destroyed. There were no injuries, but Cape Canaveral Fire Chief Pat Lee requested assistance from as far away as Jacksonville and Orlando to help extinguish the blaze.

March that same year saw the first Seafood Festival at the Port sponsored by the Cocoa Beach Area Chamber of Commerce. Now called SeaFest, this annual spring event recently celebrated its twentieth anniversary. Drawing a crowd of 35,000 seafood lovers in its first year, attendance now tops 100,000.

Industry and Cargo Continue to Grow

Although the cruise business was making a strong beginning at the Port, the commercial fishing industry and cargo were growing, as well. The scallop industry in 1984 processed one-half-million pounds of the shellfish per week. In contrast, in 1970, only 1,246 pounds of calico scallops were harvested at Port Canaveral. By 1974, the figure jumped to more than a million pounds, due to the invention of a machine that mechanically removed the meat from the shell.

Photo above: Fire aboard Scandinavian Sea
Photo left: Premier Cruise Lines' StarShip Royale

Invented by Bill Lambert, the machine could process in one day as many scallops as 1,000 workers formerly did by hand. Lambert also perfected a faster method of unloading boats by outfitting a cherry picker with a clam-shaped bucket that scooped up fifty bushels at one bite. Using this method, one machine operator could do in two hours what formerly took eight men twelve hours to do.

Machines helped process calico scallops faster and more efficiently, reducing cost and time dramatically.

In December 1984, Georgia Pacific selected Port Canaveral for its Florida lumber distribution point, moving seventy million board feet through the Port in a year. Shipments of newsprint continued, having grown from 506 tons in 1966 to 80,000 tons in 1985. A new method adopted in 1986 for moving the newsprint from the deck to the warehouse speeded up flow and lessened the jolt to the 2,000-pound rolls. The resulting increase in shipments necessitated the addition of a 40,000-square-foot warehouse to store it.

Cargo facilities, before completion of the new warehouse, boasted 2,300 feet of commercial space and cargo and freezer warehouses of almost 300,000 square feet. There were two tanker berths, a roll-on/roll-off ramp and 1,200 feet of berthing space with another pier under construction.

Then Port Authority Chairman M. M. "Buck" Buchanan summed up the Port's phenomenal progress by saying, "I have seen Port Canaveral grow from practically nothing to what it is today. I feel a tremendous responsibility for what is happening here and I want to go on record as saying that we have one of the best directors and one of the best management teams of any port, anywhere. In the past four years we have had a compound twenty-three percent growth. We have reduced taxes, built three cruise terminals, added wharves and are now starting construction of the west turning basin. This could only have been accomplished with excellent management working closely with dedicated commissioners."

Port Commissioner Dave Nisbet, who had been involved since the Port's beginning, said, "So many doubted that Port Canaveral would amount to anything. It gives me a thrill to see the results of the blood, sweat and tears poured into it. We all know now it was worth it and that those non-believers were wrong." Nisbet retired from the Board later that year and in recognition of his years of service, Shrimp Road was renamed Dave Nisbet Drive.

"I have seen Port Canaveral grow from practically nothing to what it is today. I feel a tremendous responsibility for what is happening here..."

— Chairman M. M. "Buck" Buchanan

In November 1985,

the StarShip Oceanic

arrived at Cruise Terminal 5

to join the StarShip Royale

in anticipation of beginning

regular three- and four-day

cruises to the Bahamas.

In November 1985, the *StarShip Oceanic* joined the *StarShip Royale* in anticipation of beginning regular three- and four-day cruises to the Bahamas. The expected economic impact of the two ships in 1986 was $240 million.

The year 1986 began tragically with the loss of the Space Shuttle Challenger and the seven-astronaut crew in January. Port Canaveral played host to dozens of vessels involved in the recovery mission that followed.

Port Achieves Economic Independence: Ad Valorem Taxes Are Abolished

The year was an historic one for the Port and for Brevard County for yet another reason: In June, commissioners voted to eliminate ad valorem taxes. Port Director Rowland said, "We are now generating sufficient revenue from customer user fees to carry our debt service and operate, maintain and continue the steady expansion of the Port without taxes. Although the Port is less than half developed, it has the momentum to continue to develop into an economic asset second only in Brevard County to the Kennedy Space Center. While doing this, we will continue to expand our recreational assets and improve our beauty."

He was correct in his analysis, for the Port remains economically self-sufficient today and has continued to expand and improve steadily. It was in October 1986 that a bid for the extension of Pier 3 on the north side from 420 feet to 700 feet was awarded. The new

pier would be capable of berthing two large ships or three smaller ones and would cost $6 million. Continued cargo growth demanded the extension with cargo tonnage expected to double every ten years.

The estimated economic impact of the Port on East Central Florida in 1986 was $340 million. The projected income for the Port in fiscal year 1987 was $7.1 million, of which $3.2 million would be directly related to the cruise industry. Income in 1986 from ships, passengers and cargo surpassed the previous year by sixty-three percent. By 1988, cargo tonnage had increased to 261 million tons, worth $324 million; and by 1989, 450,000 passengers passed through the Port's terminals. General operating revenue grew over that of the previous year by almost ten percent. And just one year later, according to a University of Central Florida study, the Port's impact on Central Florida amounted to $835 million, including 30,000 jobs and $265 million in wages.

Foreign Trade Zone 136 is Activated

In March 1987, the Port received its license for Foreign Trade Zone (FTZ) 136, the eighth such zone in Florida and the only one to offer quadramodal transportation — an interconnection between sea, land, air and space transportation. The application process for FTZ 136 had begun in January 1984 and $25,000 had been budgeted for its development.

The Zone was activated in 1989 with Astrotech Space Operations, a payload processing facility as its first customer. On June 7, 1989, a commercial "Sky Net" satellite arrived from the United Kingdom, saving the owners $328,000 in customs duties. Six months later that satellite was launched aboard a Titan rocket from Cape Canaveral Air Force Station, becoming the fastest export in history. It reached the three-mile limit (straight up) in twenty-seven seconds. *Florida Today* noted that it went "from Port Canaveral's Foreign Trade Zone to the Twilight Zone."

Dredging for expansion of the west turning basin began in 1986 in response to an increasing demand for cruise and cargo facilities. At a cost of $150 million, the project was the most important in Port Canaveral's history. It involved the removal of four million cubic yards of spoil, tripling the Port's deepwater berthing capacity to meet future shipping needs of Central Florida. The basin was planned to accommodate sixteen ship berths and up to nine terminals.

In 1987, the Port Authority concerned itself with increased security, budgeting $300,000 to upgrade security measures. "The Port is growing very fast and crime and terrorism are growing internationally," said then Board Chairman Malcolm "Mac" McLouth," in words that would prove prophetic. "Our goal is to make Port Canaveral the safest and most secure port in the world. We must be progressive and proactive and head off any incidences of terrorism, drug trafficking or theft before they occur."

By June of that year, 5,000 jobs were created by Port Canaveral operations. Only three employers in the county were larger: Kennedy Space Center with 14,000; Harris Corporation with 11,000; and Patrick Air Force Base with 6,200. Port employment was expected to surpass 10,000 in the coming five to seven years.

Photo: Sky Net satellite

Conservation and Recreation Needs Are Addressed

It also was in 1987 that Jetty Park was earmarked for extensive landscaping, new construction and upgraded facilities. The most used park in Brevard County, it had hosted more than seven million visitors. The new master plan included the planting of new trees and purchase of an additional 210 acres of land for sixty more campsites and 260 feet of beachfront.

Two years later, in January 1989, Port's End Park was dedicated. The four-acre park, the second of five that were being planned, was built at a cost of $450,000. It consisted of boat launching ramps, an observation tower, covered picnic pavilions, restrooms, a boat washing station and fish cleaning tables. The third park, Central Park, was completed in December 1990. Later named Freddie Patrick Park to honor the memory of a former Sheriff's deputy who served at the Port, it received awards from Keep Brevard Beautiful and the Cocoa Beach Area Chamber of Commerce.

Turning from recreation to conservation, discussions were begun in 1987 between the Port Authority and the Corps of Engineers concerning beach restoration. The Corps was moving forward with a study and hoped soon to have funding for placing 3.5 million cubic yards of sand later in the year. The wheels of progress often turn slowly, however, and it would be more than another decade before beach renourishment would become a reality.

Conservation remained an ever-present concern for Port officials, and in 1988 the Port Authority won an Environmental Award of Excellence from the American Association of Port Authorities (AAPA) for deepening and creating new upland areas around the perimeter of the west turning basin. The mitigation project involved enhancing the waters of Sykes Creek marsh with the installation of culverts, weirs and pumps in order to benefit wading birds and young estuarine fishes.

The Cruise Industry Continues to Grow

The cruise industry continued to boom at the Port with the arrival of a third Premier ship, the *StarShip Majestic* in March 1989. Estimates of its economic impact were for $1.4 million a year, bringing the total impact of Port Canaveral's cruise industry on East Central Florida to $350 million a year. Later that same year, Premier replaced the 1,100-passenger *StarShip Royale* with the 1,600-passenger *StarShip Atlantic*.

During 1989, cruise business grew thirty-eight percent and cargo ten percent. Operating revenue increased twenty-one percent to $9.2 million and operating income increased four percent to $4.3 million. Total revenue grew twenty percent to $9.9 million and net income saw growth to $3.9 million, an increase of fifty-seven percent.

Early in 1990, Carnival Cruise Lines homeported the *S/S Carnivale* at the Port after spending $10 million on refurbishing the ship. Later that year, the *Europa Star* moved to Port Canaveral from Jacksonville, beginning one-day cruises to nowhere. Then in March 1991, Carnival, having found financial success with its first ship at the Port, moved the *S/S Mardi Gras*,

Photo: Freddie Patrick Park boat launching ramps at sunrise.

sister ship of the *Carnivale*, to homeport at Canaveral. That year, cruise revenue went up forty-one percent to $7 million and cargo increased eleven percent, passing the three-million-ton mark for the first time.

The outstanding event of 1991 was the completion and dedication of Cruise Terminal 5. The first building in Port Canaveral's west turning basin, it was almost five times the size of terminals 2, 3 and 4. At 42,000 square feet, it had a passenger capacity of 3,000. It was the first mega-ship terminal in the United States built with a dredged, deepwater berth for the big ships then on the drawing boards. At a cost of $16 million, it was as beautiful as it was functional.

"We wanted to tell the cruise world that we're in the industry to stay," said Jerry Allender, then Chairman of the Port Authority.

The Port's fourth decade ended on a promising note for the future with the signing into law of the Water Resources Development Act. It provided funding for navigation projects and contained authorization to approve the first installment of $6.1 million for the Port's widening and deepening project in fiscal year 1993. Widening and deepening were deemed essential for increasing annual tonnage through accommodation of deeper draft vessels.

In December 1992, the Inlet Management Plan was completed. Its purpose was to evaluate the Port's impact on the adjacent beaches and to recommend a preferred course of action for restoring the natural sediment transport patterns. Five principal steps were recommended: Disposing suitable dredged material nearshore (instead of in deep water offshore) during maintenance of the inlet's entrance channel; tightening both jetties and extending the south jetty; interim nourishment of the beaches with suitable dredged material from Port expansion projects; bypassing sand from the north side of the inlet to the south side; and placement of ten million cubic yards of sand along Brevard's beaches south of the inlet to mitigate the inlet's historical erosion.

Implementation of the plan began immediately with the Corps of Engineers' adoption of nearshore disposal of dredged sand, with the remainder of the plan being implemented over the next twelve years. Port Canaveral was the first deepwater port to develop an Inlet Management Plan, and has since become internationally known for its proactive leadership in reversing the erosion caused by navigation inlets on adjacent beaches.

Port Canaveral had moved from its own humble beginnings to a driving economic force in the county, the state and even the nation. It had become the "Port of Choice" for vacationers, for shippers, for boaters, and for many small businesses that operated along its shore. Like the first export from FTZ 136, the sky was the limit as it moved steadily toward its golden anniversary.

Photo above: Cruise Terminal 5 interior
Photo left: Cruise Terminal 5 exterior

PORT CANAVERAL: CRUISE PORT OF THE 21ST CENTURY — THE FIFTH DECADE

SeaEscape received

a water-cannon salute

upon entering the Port harbor

for the first time.

P ort Canaveral began its fifth decade with a new slogan, emblazoned on a banner used at trade shows all over the world: *Cruise Port of the 21st Century*. As it turned out, that wasn't just bragging — it was prophetic.

In April 1993, one-day cruising was back with the arrival of the *S/S Scandinavian Song*. Carnival's *M/V Fantasy* arrived five months later, in September, replacing the *S/S Carnivale* and the *S/S Mardi Gras*. The presence of the larger ship increased Carnival's passenger capacity by 400 passengers per sailing.

The arrival of the *Fantasy* was facilitated by additions to Cruise Terminal 5 that included a $1.9 million high-level passenger ramp with a space shuttle viewing deck on top, and a $2 million addition of 17,000 square feet of baggage space. The parking lot also was doubled in size and bus bays for twenty buses with canopied approaches for passengers were added. Additional Customs space upgraded the terminal to handle ships with 3,500 passengers.

In May 1995, Port Commissioners signed an agreement with the new Disney Cruise Line to homeport its first luxury liner, the *Disney Magic*, at the Port, and to build Cruise Terminal 8 at an estimated cost of $22.5 million. It was to be the first cruise terminal in the United States designed and built to a particular cruise line's specifications and for its exclusive use. The deal was the culmination

Photo right: Carnival Fantasy at daybreak

of years of "romancing the mouse," and Mickey was there for the signing ceremony, all decked out in his white captain's uniform from his early days as Steamboat Willie.

In December 1995, Cruise Terminal 9/10 opened with 1,500 people in attendance. The party was co-hosted by the Cocoa Beach Area Chamber of Commerce as a fund-raiser and it turned out to be the most successful, one-day benefit in their history. Then Commission Chairman Malcolm "Mac" McLouth remarked during opening ceremonies that the goal in building Cruise Terminal 9/10, one of the most modern, passenger-friendly terminals in the industry, "was for the cruise experience to start the minute the passenger walks through the terminal door."

The beautiful building was dubbed "a berthing place fit for a queen," and rightly so, for the most famous queen in the world — the *Queen Elizabeth II* — docked there on her fourth visit to the Port a few weeks later.

Total cruise passenger count for 1995 was 557,500 people, an increase of nineteen percent over 1994. In February 1996, Cape Canaveral Cruise Line brought the *Dolphin IV* to the Port. With six passenger decks, a casino and two restaurants, it served 640 passengers and joined three other homeported ships: the *Atlantic*, the *Oceanic*, and the *Fantasy*. Early in January 1997, the *Diamond Royale* began

Photo above: Royal Caribbean International's Sovereign of the Seas
Photo left: Cruise Terminal 9/10

operating same-day gaming cruises and after four months of operation was producing more than $40,000 in revenue per month for the Port. Later that year the ship was sold to SunCruz Casinos and in May 1998, the *SunCruz VIII* was substituted for the older ship, increasing passenger capacity from 600 to 1,000.

That same month, May 1998, Mickey Mouse was back again to help dedicate the 72,000-square-foot Cruise Terminal 8. Soaring fireworks, a burst of birds flying, a red-white-and-blue veil of balloons and a cloud of shimmering pixie dust marked the moment. It was a glitzy occasion, but nothing to compare with the arrival of the *Disney Magic* two months later. A crowd of 10,000 greeted the massive ship as she was ushered in at 7:15 a.m. by ten boats flying dancing kites, two media boats, two tugboats spraying streams of colored water, three helicopters, three planes streaming banners, and a Disney yacht with Mickey and Minnie onboard. A flotilla of local boaters closed in behind the ship while its horn blasted the opening notes of "*When You Wish Upon A Star*." The grand climax came when she slid gracefully into her berth, shooting fireworks from her bow. Two weeks later, Patty Disney, wife of Roy Disney, christened the ship.

The year, 1998, marked the first seven-day cruises from the Port. The *Norwegian Crown* made two trips to Bermuda in the spring before being repositioned to South America. It also was in 1998 that Sterling Casino Lines began making twice-daily gaming cruises with the *New Yorker*. The ship was replaced the next year by the *M/V Ambassador II*, which welcomed its three-millionth guest aboard in 2003. At 440 feet, it can accommodate as many as 1,800 passengers and is said to be the world's largest gambling ship. The *SunCruz VIII* celebrated the boarding of its millionth guest during the summer of 2002 and in the fall of 2003, replaced the ship with the 1,200-passenger *Surfside Princess*.

The 20th Century drew to a close with the arrival of Disney's second ship, the *Disney Wonder*, in August. She was greeted by 6,000 well-wishers. At 964 feet long, she has a capacity of 2,400 passengers and a crew of 919. Like her sister ship, her economic impact on the Central Florida area has been about $100 million a year and her arrival made Port Canaveral the undisputed second largest cruise port in the world. The *Disney Wonder* was "magically" christened in October in a twilight ceremony. Instead of the traditional bottle of champagne, pixie dust was sprinkled about her hull by a computerized laser image of Tinkerbell.

Cargo Experiences Phenomenal Growth During the Last Decade

While the cruise ships stole the glamour limelight during the 1990s, cargo remained a strong economic force at the Port. In 1993, Foreign Trade Zone 136 was ranked one of the top ten in the United States by International Business magazine. In 1994, cargo berthing space was extended by 300 feet and by 1995, a concerted effort was made to attract new cargo. Cotton

Photo above: The Disney Magic and the Disney Wonder
Photo left: The Disney Cruise Line Terminal lights up the night sky at Port Canaveral.

became a new commodity at 1,771 tons and total tonnage that year surpassed three million. In 1996, cargo tonnage increased twelve percent and the leading commodities were lumber, newsprint, bananas, petroleum, salt and cement.

In 1995, the *Sunbelt Dixie* loaded her 20 millionth citrus carton onboard bound for Japan. During the 1994-95 season, 129,607 tons of citrus were handled through the Port. Mid-Florida Freezer Warehouses, Ltd. converted 10,000 square feet of warehouse space from ambient to chill and a new 30,000-square-foot warehouse with chill/ambient storage opened in February. Another 60,000 square-foot, air-conditioned warehouse was under design for FTZ 136. It opened in 1997, operated by Integrated Distribution Services. Disney Cruise Line contracted to use 25,000 square feet of it to support its operation at the Port.

By 1997, the Port was importing or exporting about 3.5 million tons per year of bulk liquids, dry bulk, break bulk and refrigerated cargoes across eight dry cargo berths, three tanker berths and one roll-on/roll-off ramp. Cargo had grown at a rate of about five percent per year, nearly doubling since 1980. In March of 1997, an announcement was made for the construction of a new container yard. Designed to lower the cost of transportation for consumer goods and increase the competitive nature of both imports and exports, phase one had a capacity for 320 twenty-foot containers. The container yard was completed in 1998.

Photo above: Fresh grapefruit being exported to Europe
Photo right: Reefer (Refrigerated) cargo ship at sunrise

That same year, 1998, cargo increased nearly ten percent and in December, Mid-Florida Freezer installed a high-performance, mobile crane from Austria, the first of its kind in the United States. It was used to load and unload containers and break bulk cargoes. Its lifting capacity was 88,400 pounds, four times as great as that of a ship's crane. In addition, it moved much faster, providing the ability to handle more cargo per hour.

Sand Bypass System Becomes a Reality

Eager to continue the work outlined in the Inlet Management Plan, the Port, in 1993, placed 100,000 cubic yards of sand that had been dredged to create Cruise Terminal 8 along a mile of the City of Cape Canaveral shoreline. Then early in 1994, the Port installed a 500-foot-long, sand-filled, geotextile tube along the south jetty to block the loss of sand from Jetty Park into the inlet. These interim measures were implemented while

awaiting the Corps of Engineers' sand bypass project and permanent improvements to the jetties.

In August 1994, a groundbreaking ceremony was held at Cruise Terminal 4 for the long-awaited sand bypass system and the work actually began in January 1995. The project renourished another two and one-quarter miles of beach in Cape Canaveral. About 636,000 cubic yards of sand were pumped from the north side of the inlet to the beaches south of the inlet's south jetty, widening the beach by about fifty feet. Authorized by Congress in 1962, the project had been delayed more than thirty years.

Extension and tightening of the south jetty and creation of a fishing pier began in late 1994 as part of the mitigation process for preservation of the shoreline. At the same time, the extension was turned into a recreational asset for the public, creating a smooth, concrete fishing pier that was lighted at night, and lengthened from 700 feet to 1,200 feet.

Named the Malcolm E. McLouth Fishing Pier, it honored the then commissioner, and now Port Director, who had pressed for the sand bypass and beach renourishment program for twenty-eight years. "The one man, however, who was really responsible for the beach restoration program," says McLouth, "was Bob Murkshe. He was an old friend and the mayor of Cocoa Beach for a number of years, and he convinced me early on that somehow the jetties played a major role in the beach erosion problem. He deserves credit, even now years after his death, because he lobbied government at all levels for those beaches. He laid all the groundwork and was tireless in his efforts. Later, Port Commissioner Ralph Kennedy took up

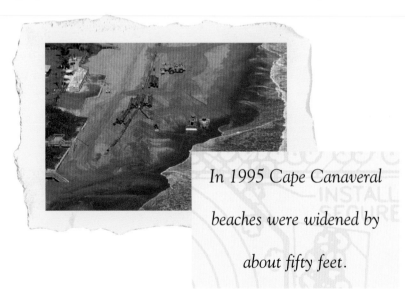

In 1995 Cape Canaveral beaches were widened by about fifty feet.

Photo right: Jetty Park's Malcolm E. McLouth Fishing Pier at twilight

Sea oats are a vital part of the beach and give the sand dunes much needed protection.

the gauntlet and lobbied for the beach projects, pursuing them relentlessly. Without the two of them, it never would have happened."

Parks and Recreation
Are Improved and Developed

Conservation and recreation in other areas also progressed during the last decade of the century. The Port won a Community Involvement Environmental Award in 1995 from the American Association of Port Authorities for giving away 65,000 sea oat and bitter panicum plants to the public for planting along Brevard County beaches. The plants helped to control erosion of dunes and provided food and cover for birds, small wildlife and nesting sea turtles.

Also in 1995, the Port took back the operation and development of Jetty Park. Plans for improvements to Jetty Park included additional parking, new and upgraded campsites and new landscaping. A $9 million project, it is ongoing at this time and is about half completed. "The Port wants to become a destination, not just a location," Commissioners said, in unveiling the plans.

Continuing its efforts in beach restoration, Canaveral Port Authority, in 1996, placed 40,000 cubic yards of sand from an upland commercial source onto the severely eroded shoreline of Cocoa Beach at Minutemen Causeway. At the same time, the Port was working diligently for the implementation of large-scale restoration of Brevard's beaches by the Corps of Engineers.

The space shuttle launches have been a major attraction in the Port Canaveral area for years.

In 2000, a $200,000 manatee protection system was installed at the Canaveral Lock. Sensors with emitters and receivers create beams that are interrupted when a manatee passes through the gates. When one of the "gentle giants" interrupts at least two beams, an alarm is activated that stops the gate. The Port Authority also initiated installation of a new sewage pump-out station for boaters on the Barge Canal. The station and other measures taken throughout the year ensure the quality of the water will continue to sustain boaters and wildlife, as well as industry.

Marketing, Public Relations and Development Are Important Areas of Growth

The phenomenal success that marked Port Canaveral during the 1990s did not take place without three vital areas of growth: marketing, public relations and infrastructure. In March 1996, the Port went high-tech, adding a website, email addresses and a toll free phone number to its communications tools. Nine months later, the website had recorded over seven million hits.

In 1996, Port Canaveral adopted a sister port — Zeeland Seaports in the Netherlands. A major portion of the Port's fresh and frozen citrus shipments destined for Europe are routed through Zeeland, so the relationship was a natural. A delegation from Port Canaveral visited their Dutch "relatives," receiving a welcome suited to a valued member of the family and a bronze plaque that is affixed to the front of the Administrative Building at Port Canaveral.

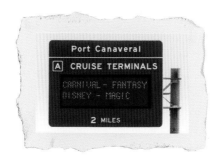

Community involvement continued to be a priority at the Port, as evidenced by the day of activity that marked the return to space of Senator John Glenn on October 29, 1998. Port commissioners, assisted by the Cocoa Beach Area Chamber of Commerce, hosted people from dawn to dusk at Cruise Terminal 9/10 to celebrate the historic launch. The day began with breakfast for NASA's VIP guests before they boarded buses for the launch-viewing site. The next wave of guests was much more exuberant when four hundred gifted students from across the United States and Canada arrived to view the launch from the terminal and to enjoy box lunches. The day ended when the VIP guests returned by bus from the launch area for a reception at the terminal.

Bigger ships, larger cargoes and more people need roads as well as terminals and warehouses, and Port Canaveral did not neglect that area of expansion during the 1990s. In 1995, design work began on the new State Road 528/George King Boulevard interchange, with construction beginning in the fall of 1999. The project involved re-routing George King Boulevard, reworking the utilities and re-routing storm water drainage from the Banana River. The new single-point interchange was designed to be a cross between a tight urban interchange and an expansive cloverleaf. The first of its kind in the county, the new bridge was designed of precast concrete reinforced with an earth retaining wall system. It was finished in 2002.

Another aid to cruise passengers was added in 1999 with electronic signs erected along State Road 528, guiding guests to their destination. Port Canaveral has met great success as a "drive-to" port, which has helped it to develop into the major cruise destination it is today. Creating a vacation mentality even before the passenger arrives at the terminal has helped in that process.

Work also began in the Canaveral Cove area: the reconstruction of roads, with curbs, gutters, sidewalks, off-street parking, underground utilities and landscaping. The Port spent $44,000 on such improvements in 1995, and in 1996, initiated a $2-million-per-year construction program that would continue through the end of the century. In February 1997, Canaveral Cove was opened with a "Splash Bash" sponsored by the Cove restaurants: Rusty's, Lloyd's, Frankie's Wings and Things and Schoolie's.

Safety and security were not neglected by Port Canaveral during these years of accelerated growth and change. A new maritime firefighter training facility was built at a cost of $1.5 million. It resembles a ship, complete with a simulated bulkhead and pier and it gives firefighters a realistic experience in training. At 154 feet long, thirty-seven feet wide and twenty-five feet high, it has three levels. It was constructed out of container boxes put together like Legos. It has a bow and stern, portholes, chains, anchors and watertight doors. Computer simulators generate a variety of kinds of onboard fires. The first students to use the new simulator were enrolled in September 1998.

Photo left: Canaveral Cove at twilight
Photo above: Electronic changeable message signs on State Road 528

$276 million impact on the Central Florida region, with cargo responsible for a $27 million direct impact.

These figures indicated a growth of twenty percent since the last economic impact study was completed in 1993. The bottom line: Port Canaveral has an $808 million impact for the eleven-county Central Florida region; for the state of Florida, a $1.6 billion impact; and for the nation, a $2 billion impact.

Military Presence at the Port Continues to be Important

In March 2001, the *USS Wasp*, the largest naval ship ever to dock at the Port, arrived for the weekend. At 844 feet long and with a beam width of 106 feet, it can land helicopters and vertical/short take-off aircraft on its flight deck, and can propel Marine landing forces into the sea for an assault on a hostile beach. A year later, the new Coast Guard Cutter *Shrike* entered service in official ceremonies at the Port. Keynote speaker at the event was Congressman Dave Weldon, whose wife, Nancy, is the ship's sponsor. The vessel employs the latest technological advances in navigation and marine technology and its role at the Port encompasses homeland security, search and rescue operations and environmental protection.

A highlight of spring 2003 was the commissioning of the nation's newest warship, the *USS Mason* at Port Canaveral. It was a day filled with pride for

Closing out the century, a highlight was the commissioning of the *USS Porter*, (DDG78), Freedom's Champion, on March 20, 1999. It was the first naval ship commissioning ever held at Port Canaveral with 5,600 guests attending the ceremony.

A New Century Dawns

The dawn of a new century ushered in an era of continued prosperity for Port Canaveral. Early in the new year, the University of Central Florida published its economic study of the Port. It revealed that in 1999, more than 15,000 people in Brevard County worked at the Port, earning about $304 million in wages. Regionally, the number totaled 30,000, with workers taking home $504 million in wages. The cruise industry accounted for a

Lt. James A. Klein,

Commanding Officer of the

Shrike was congratulated

by Nancy Weldon,

sponsor of the ship.

many – from the ship's builders and the Navy's high command to the throng of thousands who cheered her as she cruised past the jetties. Her arrival was celebrated and marked by activities steeped in patriotism and Naval tradition.

Rowland Retires and McLouth Takes the Helm

The biggest events of 2000 happened in June, November and December. In June, Charles "Chuck" Rowland retired after twenty years as Port Director. More than 400 people attended a party in his honor at Cruise Terminal 9/10 where he learned that the road connecting the three mega-ship terminals had been named for him. When he came to the Port, he saw it as "putty to be molded." There were ten employees at that time, but when he left there were 150. He brought the Port into the 21st Century with his drive and dedication and left it in capable hands, with the selection of Malcolm "Mac" McLouth to run the show. McLouth, who had been on the Port Authority Board for twenty-nine and a half years, had resigned from the commission four years earlier, in 1996, to become the Port's Deputy Director of Marketing and Trade Development.

Beach Renourishment, the New Intermodal Gate and Increased Security Mark the End of the Port's Fifth Decade

Beach renourishment was the headline event in November 2000, when a ceremony beachside celebrated the beginning of the sand transfer by

Photo left: The USS Mason received a water-cannon salute as she entered the harbor.

Security has become a very important part of day-to-day business at Port Canaveral.

the Corps of Engineers along 9.4 miles of shoreline from Jetty Park to Patrick Air Force Base. Phase one included 2.8 million yards of dredged sand placed along the shoreline at a cost of $25 million. Phase two was completed in April 2002 with the placement of another 1.6 million cubic yards of sand along four miles of shoreline at Indialantic/Melbourne Beach at a cost of $15 million.

In December, the new South Cargo Intermodal Gate opened. A $1.7 million project, it uses a computerized fiber-optic weighing and tracking system to handle payloads and boost the Port's cargo capacity. Transportation and storage companies are able to reduce shipping costs because of increased efficiency through the new access point. The new entrance along George King Boulevard also provides ample room for trucks to make turns, easing ingress and egress at the cargo area.

September 11, 2001, will never be forgotten in the minds of all Americans and Port Canaveral did its patriotic part in November of that year. With a theme of "Keep America Afloat," a Freedom Celebration was launched with a rally and parade. Thousands lined the Jetty Park shoreline with small American flags and thousands more waved back from a parade of cruise ships sailing by.

New Mega-Ships Arrive

In May 2000, the 73,192-ton Royal Caribbean Cruise Line mega-ship the *Sovereign of the Seas* made its home at Port Canaveral. With a

crew of 840, it has 1,125 staterooms and can carry 2,850 passengers. In August that same year, Disney Cruise Line introduced seven-day cruises and, in September, welcomed its one-millionth guest aboard with a gala celebration.

Port Canaveral continued to make great strides forward with cargo business, even though the economy was in a "down" cycle. Mid-Florida Freezer Warehouses, at the Port since 1971, earned international recognition as the only dockside warehouse facility in the Southeastern United States to achieve International Standardization Organization (ISO) 9000 certification.

Keep America Afloat parade was held in the Port to celebrate America's freedom.

Carnival's newest mega-ship, the *Carnival Pride,* arrived in January 2001. Offering the first Western Caribbean cruises from the Port, it joined the *Carnival Fantasy,* which had been homeported at the Port since 1993. Micky Arison, Chairman of the Board, was at the Port for the arrival, as was Carnival Cruise Lines' President Bob Dickinson. There was a formal luncheon onboard, followed by the naming ceremony, during which the ship's godmother, former astronaut Dr. Tamara Jernigan, pulled the cord to break the traditional bottle of champagne.

Carnival Glory became

the largest cruise ship to

homeport at Canaveral

The ship carries 2,667 passengers and has 1,062 staterooms, eighty percent of which offer ocean views. But before the year was out, the cruise line announced that the *Carnival Glory*, an even larger ship, would replace the *Pride* in 2003. The new ship, a Conquest Class vessel, exceeds the *Pride's* capacity by forty percent. At a cost of $500 million, the new ship officially took up residence at her new homeport in July 2003, where she was named by her godmother, Dr. Sally Ride, America's first woman in space. During the ceremonies, Carnival's Chief Executive Officer Bob Dickinson reminisced about Carnival's relationship with the Port. "Our decision to place the *Fantasy* here," he said, "was a leap of faith in the potential of Port Canaveral, and it proved to be a very wise choice."

At about the same time, Royal Caribbean Cruise Line announced its plans to position its newest and largest cruise ship, *Mariner of the Seas*, at the Port in November 2003. The 142,000-ton Voyager Class ship accommodates 3,114 passengers. It includes a number of other innovative features, such as a rock-climbing wall; an ice skating arena; and interior staterooms with views of the Royal Promenade, a four-story shopping and entertainment boulevard that winds through the center of the ship.

Shortly after Royal Caribbean's announcement, the *Sunbelt Spirit* was welcomed to Port Canaveral with an elegant dinner on deck at the half-way point of her maiden voyage. Leaving Japan with a cargo of automobiles for delivery to points north on the Eastern Seaboard, she arrived at Port Canaveral to take on a load of refrigerated fruit cargo for her return trip to Japan. She was welcomed by Florida's First Lady, Columba Bush, who is her sponsor.

Photo above: Carnival Glory Master, Capt. Carlo Quierolo, and
former astronaut Dr. Sally Ride celebrate
the naming of the Port's newest and largest cruise ship.

Infrastructure construction during 2001 and 2002 was dictated largely by security needs imposed by the terrorist attacks on the World Trade Center and the Pentagon in 2001. Port Canaveral was recognized as the first Florida seaport to meet the new security standards set by Florida law. A patrol boat was purchased and a contract negotiated between the Port and the Brevard County Sheriff's Department. Port spending for security now amounts to $75,000 a week, or almost $4 million annually. Security at the cruise terminals has doubled, and fencing, lighting and electronic security measures have been installed.

Port Looks Forward to Continued Growth

Port Canaveral ends its first fifty years poised for continued greatness as it moves toward its own century mark. Those mega-terminals that once seemed enormous continue to shrink as more and larger ships utilize them. New baggage retrieval systems and a new, multi-level parking garage have enabled the Port to move people more efficiently. Now the second largest cruise port in the world, nearly 2,000,000 passengers will pass through its portals by the end of 2003.

Part of its greatness is due to those dedicated visionaries who have been part of its history. "Mac" McLouth, who stands at the helm now, has remarked that the commemorative streets named for them are entirely appropriate. "George King has the main boulevard," he said, "because he was the first mover and shaker to come aboard."

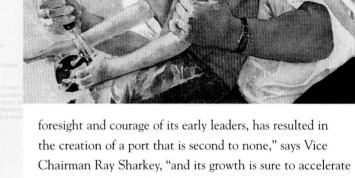

Then there was Glen Cheek, who concentrated on developing cargo and whose name graces a street in the commercial area. Next was Charles "Chuck" Rowland, whose great drive and expertise made the Port a leading cruise port in the world, and whose contributions are immortalized at the cruise terminals' connecting road on the north side. Finally, there's "Mac," who likes the fact that his tribute goes back to his first encounter with the Port as that Boy Scout leader who camped out there a long time ago: "The Malcolm McLouth Fishing Pier at Jetty Park."

Although he's the head of the Port, McLouth still pays attention to all the details involved in running the mammoth operation. On foggy mornings, he often awakes before dawn at his beachfront residence and listens to the foghorns of the cruise ships returning to port. "Each of them has a different timbre," he said, "and I know which is which. And I can't go back to sleep until I hear the horns stop and I know each ship has maneuvered the channel to its berth and is safely home."

Port Commissioners share McLouth's ever-present care and concern for the Port — both its present and its future. "The Port's accessibility to Central Florida's recreational and environmental attractions, coupled with the

Malcolm "Mac" McLouth was presented with this painting in commemoration of his tireless efforts to create Port recreational facilities for the public.

foresight and courage of its early leaders, has resulted in the creation of a port that is second to none," says Vice Chairman Ray Sharkey, "and its growth is sure to accelerate as tourism and global trade continue to expand."

Commissioner Ralph Kennedy said, "Port Canaveral has become what it was envisioned — a major economic contributor to our community and beyond. I am proud of what we have accomplished — creating opportunities and employment, for both large and small businesses. We have helped bring the world closer to Brevard County and Central Florida. What I am equally as proud of is the balance we have created between growth and the environment."

"As a lifelong Floridian and Brevard resident for 43 years," Commissioner Tom Goodson said, "I have childhood memories of Port Canaveral as a sleepy little port with most of the income coming from fishing, fuel, and restaurants. To see what the Port has developed into is nothing short of amazing. Personally I feel privileged to be able to help direct Port

Photo left: Cruise Terminal 9/10 at sunset

Canaveral into the future. I am sure it will continue to be an economic engine for Brevard County and Central Florida."

Former Board Chairman Joe Matheny said, " We must strive to bring the cargo and container trade into balance with the cruise explosion now being experienced by Port Canaveral; and we also must dedicate more of our energy and our resources to developing Brevard County business, as well as its cultural and community activities."

Like Matheny, Port Authority Board Chairman Rodney Ketcham has poured years of effort and expertise into making the Port what it is today. A resident of Cocoa Beach since the early 1950s, he remembers when there was no Port Canaveral.

"Port Canaveral, as I see it," he said, "will remain a vibrant, prosperous business community fifty years from now, offering trade and industrial job opportunities, as well as opportunities for shopping, leisurely cruise vacations and recreational activities. All of this will be contained in environmentally sensitive and secure surroundings; and the name 'Fun Port' will still apply." Such is the dedication — and determination — that has made Port Canaveral what it is today and what it will become in the future.

2003 CANAVERAL PORT AUTHORITY

Board of Commissioners

Pictured from left to right: Tom Goodson, Secretary/Treasurer; Joe D. Matheny, Commissioner; Raymond P. Sharkey, Vice Chairman; Rodney Ketcham, Chairman; Ralph J. Kennedy, Commissioner

Directors

MALCOLM E. McLOUTH, P.E.
Executive Director

WILLIAM P. BANCROFT
Deputy Executive Director of Security, Operations & Administration

ALBERT J. FRANCIS II, CPA, PPM
Chief Financial Officer/Deputy Executive Director

ROBERT GIANGRISOSTOMI
Deputy Executive Director of Business Development

RICHARD B. LOMBROIA
Chief of Engineering & Planning

JEANNIE ADAME
Director of Environmental Plans & Programs

MARK A. BLAKE
Director of Construction/Assistant Chief of Engineering & Planning

DWIGHT FENDER
Director of Operations & Maintenance

LAUREN A. KOTAS, PPM
Director of Marketing & Trade Development

DIXIE N. SANSOM
Director of Government Relations & Public Affairs

JERRY SIMON, PPM
Director of Security

MARGI STARKEY
Director of Accounting

Photo right: 21st Century aerial view of Port Canaveral

CARNIVAL CRUISE LINES

Carnival Cruise Lines has grown from a struggling one-ship operation to the world's largest and most popular cruise line, with a fleet of nineteen "Fun Ships" carrying upwards of three million passengers annually — the most in the cruise industry.

A large part of Carnival's growth has been its relationship with Port Canaveral, one of the cruise industry's fastest growing homeports popularized by its centralized location and proximity to area theme parks and attractions.

Carnival began sailing from Port Canaveral in 1990 with the 950-passenger "Fun Ship" *Carnivale* operating year-round three- and four-day Bahamas cruises.

"Fun Ship" cruising from Port Canaveral aboard the *Carnivale* proved so popular, in fact, that just one year later a second vessel, the 1,000-passenger *Mardi Gras*, was added.

Then, in an unprecedented move, Carnival replaced these two vessels in 1993 with the 2,056-passenger *Fantasy*, at the time the newest and largest ship based year-round at Port Canaveral.

The *Fantasy* was an immediate hit, consistently sailing in excess of one hundred percent capacity. Carnival continued its expansion in the Port with the deployment of the 2,124-passenger

Carnival Pride on its first-ever seven-day Caribbean cruise program from Port Canaveral in January 2002. It also marked the first time that Carnival positioned a brand new ship on the Space Coast.

Just three months after *Carnival Pride's* debut from Port Canaveral, the company announced that it would increase capacity on this route by forty percent with the deployment of the new 2,974-passenger *Carnival Glory* — the newest and largest "Fun Ship" to operate from that port — in July 2003.

In addition to serving as the departure point for thousands of satisfied Carnival guests, Port Canaveral has been the site for two of the company's most memorable naming ceremonies. Celebrated astronauts — Dr. Tamara Jernigan and Dr. Sally Ride — presided over naming ceremonies for *Carnival Pride* in 2002 and *Carnival Glory* in 2003, forever linking these vessels to Port Canaveral and the area's vital aerospace industry.

Over the past thirteen years, Carnival and Port Canaveral have experienced unprecedented growth, with the port accounting for some 400,000 Carnival passengers annually — a two hundred percent increase over 1990.

The two entities look forward to building upon their thirteen-year relationship while continuing to provide consumers with relaxing, memorable seagoing vacations from this outstanding and exceptional homeport.

Photo left: Carnivale and Mardi Gras at Port Canaveral's Cruise Terminals 2 and 3
Photo right: Carnival Glory arriving in Port Canaveral

FLORIDA TODAY
THE SPACE COAST'S NUMBER ONE SOURCE FOR NEWS AND INFORMATION

It was March 1966 and the space age was well underway in Brevard County, Florida when the first issue of Today newspaper, the forerunner of FLORIDA TODAY, rolled off the presses. Some years earlier, the Gannett Publishing Company had acquired the Cocoa Tribune, a weekly paper and the only local paper serving Central Brevard.

Recognizing the growth potential of the county, Cape Publications was formed and the old Tribune plant was enlarged and modernized to accommodate the new daily, which covered the entire county. Over the next twenty years Today continued to grow and add more products and services to meet the ever-changing needs of the community. To reflect those changing times and to broaden the scope of coverage, the name was changed in 1985 to FLORIDA TODAY.

"Our goal is to help to preserve the best traditions of this historic birthplace of the Space Age."

— *Allen H. Neuharth*

The next year, in 1986, the publication moved into its current location at Gannett Plaza, on U.S. Highway 1, north of Melbourne. A twenty-eight-acre National Wildlife Federation backyard wildlife habitat, Gannett Plaza is a safe haven for the birds, animals, reptiles and plants that have always made their home there. Surrounded by nine satellite dishes, the facility is an impressive 191,000-square-foot building made of glass and steel.

As a member of the Gannett Company's extensive list of daily newspapers, the facility also is one of more than thirty print sites for USA Today, the nation's newspaper. It is in operation twenty-four hours a day, seven days a week, fifty-two weeks a year. In addition to Gannett Plaza, the newspaper has bureau offices in Titusville, Palm Bay, Merritt Island and Sebastian.

In addition to reporting the daily news, Cape Publications publishes five weekly, three biweekly, and two monthly community newspapers that are tailored for distinct geographical areas within the county. These publications, which are delivered to subscribers of FLORIDA TODAY, also can be picked up free of charge at a number of distribution points throughout the area. They provide localized information and interesting features about the places and people residents know best — their neighbors.

The company's website, floridatoday.com, serves as the news and information source for an online audience. Here users find the stories which affect them in the areas of news, business, sports, entertainment and lifestyle interests, as well as a marketplace of advertising, including classifieds.

Although the Space Coast has undergone many changes during the past thirty-eight years, the mission of FLORIDA TODAY remains the same now as when Allen H. Neuharth, the founder of the newspaper, started the business in March 1966. "Our goal," he said, "is to help to preserve the best traditions of this historic birthplace of the Space Age and to help ensure that all Brevard County will realize the full potential for its bright tomorrow."

It was in this vein that FLORIDA TODAY produced a special section saluting Port Canaveral on its twenty-fifth anniversary in 1978, and takes pride in being a part of its golden anniversary celebration in 2003.

Photo: FLORIDA TODAY through the years

GEE & JENSON
A DIVISION OF CH2M HILL
ENGINEERS-ARCHITECTS-PLANNERS

G ee & Jenson, one of the state's oldest and most distinguished engineering and architectural firms, celebrated its fiftieth anniversary in 2001. From what was originally a two-man office with a couple of desks facing each other, the company grew to the eighth largest port facilities design firm in the United States with 200 employees and annual revenues of more than $19.5 million.

Herb Gee and Ted Jenson met when both were working for the U.S. Army Corps of Engineers in Jacksonville. Seeing the opportunities offered in the rapidly developing Sunshine State, they moved to West Palm Beach and set up shop. They began with land planning and water management and still are leaders in these fields today. Almost immediately, they were hired by the Old Plantation Water Control District in Broward County, and the Flood Control District which is now South Florida Water Management District.

Another early project of vital importance in the 1950s was getting a fresh water supply to Cape Canaveral to help support growth of the developing space program. The water came from Orlando and during the process, engineers connected residential homes along the way. Drinking water had been confined to sulfur wells and the taste and smell were incredibly bad.

Gee & Jenson is one of the state's oldest and most distinguished engineering and architectural firms.

Photo left top: Ted Jenson (left) and Fred Greene (right) on one of the many trips to Central Florida for the Disney project.
Photo left bottom: Founders Herb Gee and Ted Jenson met in the Army Corps of Engineers and created Gee & Jenson in 1951.
Photo right top: Fred Greene joined Gee & Jenson in 1956 and was the lead engineer for the Disney project.
Photo right bottom: Herb Gee and Ted Jenson point to a map of the Magic Kingdom.

Gee & Jenson Meets
a Famous Mouse and His Friends

A big break for the young engineering firm came in 1965 when Gee, Jenson and their top engineer, Fred Greene, were summoned to Miami to consult with officials about a mysterious job called "Project X." The men they met that day were interested "in developing some land," they said, and offered the three $5,000 to study the site and get back to them in forty-five days.

According to Greene, they covered the site in an airplane and used cameras with 180-degree lenses. "We took a lot of pictures," he said, "and Colonel Gee even canoed the streams. We reported back that they could develop 17,000 acres of the 27,000 in the parcel. We didn't know it at the time, but Walt Disney had already decided that if he could get 3,000 usable acres out of it, he would build his Magic Kingdom. So he was delighted with our report."

Gee & Jenson staff worked on the project for a couple of months before learning that "Project X" was to be Walt Disney World; and as the project began to take shape, they continued to work with Disney as the head civil engineers in developing the theme park. It stands out as one of

the company's most challenging assignments because there were so many innovative systems to design. In addition to laying out the gigantic parking lot for 13,200 cars, they designed Bay Lake and the roadway tunnel beneath the lakes connecting the entrance to the theme park.

"Bay Lake," said Greene, "was the color of iced tea and Disney wanted it clear. So Herb Gee devised a system which involved dredging the sand out of the lake, building beaches all the way around the periphery of it and raising the water surface in the lake about one foot higher so there would always be an outflow of water." In essence, the water actually was pumped out of the lake and put back in.

The company not only had to be innovative in its approach to unique design problems, it had to be fast. "When they picked an opening date, they didn't ask us if we could do it in time," said Greene. "They just said, 'We're going to open,' and we didn't argue. If we had, we would have been quickly replaced." Other projects they designed included the Golf Resort Hotel and engineering for the Palm & Magnolia Golf Courses and the Wilderness Camp Ground.

The Disney project was exciting and gave the company valuable exposure. But it didn't affect the attention the company gave to its port work and other land development projects and most of the same clients it had back then still are with the firm today.

The Disney project was exciting and gave the company valuable exposure.

The Company Expands Its Scope

In 1975, Gee & Jenson added architecture and planning to its services and developed state-of-the-art technology that included modular public safety facilities, libraries, industrial and office buildings, and cruise terminals. Recently, they completed an expansion-renovation at a Tampa cruise terminal that has become recognized as one of the fastest people-moving facilities in the industry.

In January 2002, the company merged with CH2M HILL, Inc. Prior to the merger, Gee & Jenson was well-known for excellence in port facilities planning, design and management and the merger allowed the company to expand beyond its current geographic markets and offer more services to its clients.

According to Bud Ahearn, President of CH2M HILL, the corporate cultures of the two companies were a good match, as each is entirely employee-owned and each shares similar philosophies concerning commitment to clients and encouragement of innovation in the workforce.

After the merger, Gee & Jenson was able to expand its Florida base which included the 45,000 square-foot headquarters in West Palm Beach and regional offices in Tampa, Manatee/Sarasota, Jacksonville, Coral Springs and Cape Canaveral to now include the vast outwork of over one hundred CH2M HILL offices worldwide. This expanded base will now allow Gee & Jenson to cover its nationwide range of port clients from offices the ports are located in.

Photo left: The Magic Kingdom under construction in 1970, a year before opening.

Gee & Jenson serves nearly every deep water port in Florida, beginning with the Port of Palm Beach in 1953 and Port Canaveral in 1954. The firm also has developed important relationships with all the major cruise lines, further enhancing its value to the ports they serve.

The company offers services ranging from marketing feasibility studies to engineering to facility design-build throughout the United States and in the Caribbean, Mexico and Central America. In addition, the firm already was examining port security issues prior to the terrorist attacks of September 11, 2001 and was able to assist three Florida ports obtain the Florida Department of Law Enforcement's (FDLE) "substantially compliant" designation.

Gee & Jenson Are Early Contributors to Port Canaveral's Development

The shape and structure of Port Canaveral today is due largely to Gee & Jenson's studies during the early years. They were responsible for the first master plan, and have worked diligently through the years to maintain the fine balance made necessary by the unique elements at work at this quadramodal port.

Joe LaPolla, who was Director of Engineering at the Port for twenty-two years until his recent retirement, especially values their contributions to the development of the facility. "Throughout the years," he says, "from the early development of the Port to the current work and future planning, Gee & Jenson has been an outstanding asset with the expertise to construct and maintain both cruise and cargo operations."

Phil Crannell, formerly Chairman of the Board for Gee & Jenson and now Director of Ports Practice for CH2M HILL, has been with the company for twenty-eight years. He was born and grew up in Titusville, so he knows the Port and Brevard County from a native's perspective as well as from a port expert's perspective. "We have been partners from the beginning," he says, and it has been a mutually beneficial relationship. Before there was any Port staff, we were helping to provide solutions for their environmental initiatives along with their commercial operations. It was key that we help them maintain a deep inlet and, at the same time, preserve the natural resources of the seashore."

He also notes the importance of the military issue with the presence of the Coast Guard and the Naval Ordinance Training Unit (NOTU) that support the nation's Trident Submarine program and NASA. "When we designed the Trident turning basin, our over-riding goal was to help the Port facilitate these military missions and pursue their own commercial objectives in harmony."

David Mock, Southeast Regional Ports Leader for CH2M HILL, has been with Gee & Jenson since 1974. He was the company's primary contact for Port Canaveral back then and was the lead designer for the Trident project. "In 1974, the Port got a grant from the Economic Development Administration (EDA)

Photo top: Phil Crannell, Director of Ports Practice for CH2M HILL
Photo bottom: David Mock, Southeast Regional Ports Leader for CH2M HILL, was the primary contact for Port Canaveral in the early 1970s during the Trident project.

for developing the north side of the Port, and we did all the planning for Tanker Berth number three as well as the Trident docks," he says. "We designed the west turning basin and developed the spoil areas as a conservation move; and just about every week, I would fly up to the Merritt Island Airport and Port Director George King would pick me up and drive me to the job site."

Crannell is proud of the quality of their work at Port Canaveral. "It has the reputation for being one of the finest in the United States," he said. "This can be credited to a combination of teamwork among staff and elected officials who have great vision and Gee & Jenson's ability to translate that vision into reality using the best architectural and engineering tools available."

He also points to his firm's business relationship with Disney enterprises as being a contributing factor in bringing Disney Cruise Line to the Port. "Disney knew we were capable of evaluating all the operations issues involved in getting their ships into their berths at this port. They also had confidence in our master plan for Castaway Cay, their private island. We were responsible for developing the island's facilities so they would be safe for the passengers and also for making sure the harbor would be accessible to the ship as many days during the year as possible."

The Disney terminal itself presented a number of unique challenges to the Gee & Jenson design team. They had to create land on which

Photo: Port Canaveral's Cruise Terminal 9/10

Gee & Jenson, now a part of

CH2M HILL, Inc., has served

the people of Florida well.

the terminal would sit, utilizing sands salvaged from the dredging operation. The schedule did not permit time for complete settlement of the new fill and part of the required bulkhead wall was installed on this new land. Consequently, as the contractor began installing the sheet piles using vibrating hammers, the entire wall would "walk" down the embankment. Gary Ledford, Gee & Jenson's senior project manager, designed a solution by substituting longer sheet piles that had been earmarked for another use for every fourth pair. These piles could be driven into a deeper material, creating a "picket fence" below ground level that provided the necessary stability for the entire wall. The solution was innovative, safe, and of equal importance to the client, did not increase the cost of construction nor slow it down.

Port Canaveral's Modern Terminals Reflect Gee & Jenson's Expertise

Gee and Jenson has supplied the engineering design for all the cruise terminals constructed during the last decade at Port Canaveral. Among these was the Port's first north-side terminal, Cruise Terminal 5, the first of the Port's second-generation cruise terminals, built in the mid-1990s for the Fantasy-class vessels. Then in 2001, the company provided the structural engineering for mooring and gangway improvements at this same terminal, upgrading its capability to handle the new Spirit-class cruise ships that are one hundred feet longer than the Fantasy-class vessels. Cruise Terminal 9/10, completed in 1995 to accommodate the mega-ship class liners, also benefited from the experience and

Photo: Corporate Headquarters of Gee & Jenson, a Division of CH2M HILL

innovative talents of Gee & Jenson engineers. The pier was designed to accommodate 2,600- to 3,000-passenger ships with the ability to be expanded to accommodate 3,800-passenger vessels. The extremely tight site required that the terminal be located very close to the pier, so in order to avoid potential interference between land-side and water-side structures, the pier was designed to act integrally with the bulkhead wall system, thereby eliminating the tie-back wall system usually necessary for anchored bulkheads.

When the site was expanded in 2003 to accommodate the larger ships, Gee & Jenson again provided the engineering design for expanding the existing pier. They also managed the design and construction of an elevated 3,500-square-foot enclosed access ramp to the passenger gangways. This terminal and pier will accommodate the world's largest cruise ships, the Mariner-class vessels. The completed complex of Gee & Jenson cruise terminals, made possible by the Port's visionary political officials and the solid leadership of Port staff, has resulted in the Canaveral Port Authority being ranked as the number two cruise port in the world.

Gee & Jenson, now a part of CH2M HILL, Inc., has served the people of Florida well. Its leadership during the past fifty years has contributed greatly to the economic growth and development of the state and to the conservation of its natural resources, as well.

Photo: Port Canaveral's Cruise Terminal 8 (Disney Cruise Terminal)

HOYMAN DOBSON & COMPANY, P.A.
CERTIFIED PUBLIC ACCOUNTANTS

Hoyman Dobson & Company first began serving Brevard County in 1964. The race to space was literally putting the county on the map and the area was poised for phenomenal growth. The young firm quickly became part of that growth, basing their firm on cultivating long-lasting business relationships and delivering quality client services. "Our vision," says Chas Hoyman, Managing Director of the firm, "has always been to be the best CPA firm in Central Florida by providing the greatest value to our clients."

Those clients range from small businesses to some of the largest privately held corporations in the area. Roger Dobson founded the firm in 1964 with Chas Hoyman and Gene Bjerning joining the firm in the early 70s, Barbara Oswalt and Tom Kirk joined in the early 80s with Karen Kirkland and Debbie Bradley joining in the late 80s. Although the staff has grown significantly through the years, each client still receives the same personal, individualized attention. Staff members provide a broad range of expertise and experience in a wide range of specialized accounting areas. From minimizing tax liabilities to handling mergers and acquisitions, as well as auditing and government cost accounting, the firm has the ability to handle all business-planning needs.

One of the firm's largest clients is Port Canaveral. "Back in 1977," says Hoyman, "when we first began

doing their auditing, the Port's financial resources were only a fraction of what they are today. Port Canaveral has grown into a strong economic force in the entire Central Florida region and we think our customized services have been a significant contributing factor to that growth."

Roger Dobson, Chas Hoyman and Gene Bjerning remember being a part of an exciting milestone at the young Port — the inaugural voyage of Port Canaveral's first cruise ship, the *Scandinavian Sea*. They were aboard for its first "cruise to nowhere" in February 1982 and, remembering back to that time, they find it hard to believe what they see happening at Port Canaveral today, less than twenty-five years later.

Hoyman Dobson & Company points to the Port with pride and a sense of accomplishment in the part it has played in the Port's development. The firm is particularly pleased to share in the recognition the Port's finance department has received from the Government Finance Officers Association of the United States and Canada. For the past eleven years, this organization has awarded Port Canaveral its Certificate of Achievement of Excellence in Financial Reporting (CAFR).

While this prestigious accounting firm is proud to stand on its past record of growth and community service, it is always looking to the future, as well. In the ever changing and evolving economy of the world today, Hoyman Dobson & Company continues to add

to its services to meet the needs of Central Florida businesses. Toward that end, the firm added a subsidiary branch to its existing operations in 1995 — CPA Wealth Management Services. Recognizing the financial needs that emerge with a population that is living longer and healthier lives, the firm offers investment services and money management expertise to a growing number of companies and individuals in the area.

All of the principals of the firm have been committed to the growth and stability of the local business community throughout their careers. Bjerning joined Dobson in the mid-seventies in promoting the growing tourist industry in the county. Envisioning the economic windfall this might one day become for the region, the two branched out into the hotel business —

first with the Best Western Oceanfront Resort and Days Inn and later with the Hampton Inn and Courtyard by Marriott, all located in Cocoa Beach.

All members of the firm have been heavily involved in developing Brevard County in a variety of ways. Dobson served as County Commissioner during the 1980s. Both Dobson and Bjerning have served as chairmen of the Cocoa Beach Area Chamber of Commerce; and Bjerning and Hoyman have chaired the Brevard Economic Development Commission of Florida's Space Coast.

Hoyman Dobson & Company is justifiably proud of the part it has played in shaping the past and is equally committed to an even brighter and better future.

Photo left: The Hoyman Dobson director's early years. Pictured left to right (front row) Barbara Oswalt, Karen Kirkland; (back row) Gene Bjerning, Tom Kirk, Roger Dobson and Chas Hoyman: Debbie Bradley (not shown)
Photo above: The Hoyman Dobson & Company team

MID-FLORIDA FREEZER WAREHOUSES, LTD.
DRY, CHILL AND FREEZER STORAGE AND DISTRIBUTION SERVICES

Since 1975, Mid-Florida Freezer has been operating at Port Canaveral and has grown from one 60,000-square-foot warehouse to a complex of warehouses at the Port and in Orlando. Port Canaveral facilities now include 570,000 square-feet of freezer, chilled and dry warehouse storage. The Orlando site has 525,000 square-feet of refrigerated and dry storage. The company has eighty-five full-time employees and can have over two hundred people working on a busy shipping day.

The original warehouse was owned by Tropicana, the fruit juice company. When Mid-Florida Freezer acquired the facility, the company immediately outfitted the warehouse with all new refrigeration capability, and the first products stored and shipped from the warehouse were orange juice concentrate, beef, and lamb, all imported from Brazil.

In 1982, the company acquired a 90,000-square-foot building at the Port designed to store newsprint, opening the door for a whole new market at Port Canaveral. For more than twenty years, a large part of the newsprint needed by newspapers throughout Central and South Florida has arrived via the Port and Mid-Florida Freezer.

A major export for the company has been fresh grapefruit heading to the orient. Between 1978 and 2002, more than ten million cartons of Florida fruit have been shipped from Port Canaveral to a lucrative market of consumers in Japan. Dan Richey, former Chairman of the Florida Citrus Commission, credits this lucrative market to the superior fruit and the ability of Mid-Florida Freezer to accommodate chill and load hundreds of thousands of cartons onto a ship in a matter of hours. It is this dedication to proper storage of goods and quick turn-around of the products it receives from land and sea that account for the company's success. "We are ever aware that time is money," says company president Rhonda Lee, "and we are customer focused. We strive to satisfy the unique needs of each individual customer."

The facility at Port Canaveral is close to all major markets in Florida, saving shipping days and thousands of land miles compared to northern ports. The company works to keep storage and handling costs competitive because they know shippers have alternative ways of moving their cargo.

Careful handling is part of the package every customer receives from a contract with Mid-Florida Freezer. Leading perishable shippers from the Americas, Japan and Europe praise the company for its capabilities. The facilities offer on-dock fumigation under supervision of the United States Department of Agriculture in addition to pallet netting machines to keep cargo intact and in good condition. In addition, there are automatic housekeeping machines to maintain a high level of cleanliness, both in and out of the warehouses.

Photo above: Patrick "Pat" Lee, General Partner of Mid-Florida Freezer Warehouses, inspects grapefruit destined for Japan in 1984.
Photo right: The vast array of Mid-Florida Freezer's dockside cargo handling equipment at Port Canaveral facilitates the rapid movement of products between ships and warehouses.

The company constantly is devising ways to improve handling of cargo that will reduce paperwork and provide customers with better control of their products. It strives to stay on the cutting edge of technology so that pallet by pallet or box by box, a product is tracked when it arrives, when it's stored, and when it's loaded in ship, truck or rail car. The company knows the exact location of each product all the way to its destination; and, throughout the receiving, moving and shipping processes, hand-held, wireless data terminals are used to scan bar code labels and update database records.

Mid-Florida Freezer has capitalized on Port Canaveral's central location and the easy transition it affords between land and sea transportation; and, in turn, the company has had a major impact on the Port's phenomenal growth during its first fifty years.

OLSEN ASSOCIATES, INC.
COASTAL ENGINEERING

Olsen Associates, located in Jacksonville, Florida was established in 1982 by its President, Erik J. Olsen, and the firm's management includes its Vice-President, Dr. Kevin R. Bodge, along with a staff of competent professional engineers with advance degrees in coastal and oceanographic engineering. The firm specializes in the study, design, permitting and management of projects located in coastal, insular and estuarine environments.

The firm focuses strictly on engineering problems in the coastal and nearshore environment in order to provide for its clients the most highly-developed expertise in these areas. To accomplish this, the firm strives to combine extensive experience in traditional engineering practice with leading-edge academic theory. Olsen Associates is widely respected for its successful formulation of shore protection, navigation and oceanfront development projects that are both constructible and cost-effective.

The firm specializes in the study, design, permitting and management of projects located in coastal, insular and estuarine environments.

Their record includes challenging projects constructed throughout the southeastern United States, the Caribbean, Mexico and Hawaii. The firm's professional staff is recognized internationally for their contributions to technical literature and coastal engineering design manuals and for their innovative project designs.

Among these are the first full-scale use of imported aragonite sand for beach nourishment in the United States; unique application of tuned coastal structures for shoreline stabilization; comprehensive planning and implementation of measures to minimize sand losses to ocean inlets; seabed rehandling areas for dredged material; improved geometries for beach fill profiles; mathematical modeling of shoreline changes and storm protection for oceanfront development; analysis of set-back policies for oceanfront development; and the world's first large-scale structural rehabilitation of coral reefs damaged by vessels.

When the Canaveral Port Authority first addressed the problem of inlet-related beach erosion in 1991, they looked to the experienced engineers of Olsen Associates to help them formulate an Inlet Management Plan. This plan — the first of its kind for a deepwater port in Florida — identified fifteen specific project elements to eliminate the inlet's diversion of sand from the beaches and to restore the adjacent, eroded shorelines.

Photo left: Sand bypass project
Photo right: Aerial view of beach renourishment
Photo right above: South jetty interim sand tightening

To implement the plan, the Canaveral Port Authority and Olsen Associates guided a complex effort that required the cooperation of the United States Army Corps of Engineers, the State of Florida, Brevard County, the United States Air Force, the Cities of Cape Canaveral and Cocoa Beach, and many other agencies. The plan recommended nearshore disposal of sand dredged from the inlet; interim and permanent sand-tightening and extension of the inlet jetties; sand bypassing across the jetties; and large-scale nourishment of Brevard's beaches using sand from offshore areas.

In formulating the plan, Olsen engineers introduced new methods of analysis to measure the impact of beach erosion caused by the inlet and jetties at Canaveral Harbor. They discovered that this impact was far greater than expected, in both volume and shoreline length; and their findings provided strong evidence that inlet dredging and jetties are a principal cause of beach erosion. Their techniques for analysis at Port Canaveral have since become standard, state-of-the-art tools in inlet sand management, and their conclusions have since been upheld by independent studies and court settlements.

As of 2003, the Port Canaveral Inlet Management Plan has reduced the inlet's impact to the beaches by about eighty percent, and more than seventeen miles of shoreline have been restored with more than four million cubic yards of sand. Olsen Associates, Inc. has helped the Port to become an internationally recognized leader in proactive inlet sand management.

1941-2003
CANAVERAL PORT AUTHORITY COMMISSIONERS

The original Port Charter (1939) established a seven-member board of port commissioners. These members were Port Commissioners by virtue of being elected as County Commissioners and Mayors. Only two were elected as Port Commissioners. The 1953 Charter established a five-member elected Board. The Governor appointed the first five-member board in June 1953, with elections then being held during regular elections that year.

1941-1942 A. Fortenberry *(County Commissioner)*, John Witter, W.B. Lewis, A. A. Dunn *(County Commissioner)*, R. L. Geiger *(Mayor of Rockledge)*, W. G. Akridge, W. C. Klingensmith

1943-1944 Fortenberry *(County Commissioner)*, Dunn *(County Commissioner)*, F.H. MacFarland, Geiger *(Mayor of Rockledge)*, Witter, Lewis, Noah B. Butt *(Mayor of Cocoa)*

1945 Fortenberry *(County Commissioner)*, Dunn *(County Commissioner)*, Geiger *(Mayor of Rockledge)*, S. L. Knutson, Klingensmith, Lewis, MacFarland

1946 Fortenberry *(County Commissioner)*, Geiger *(Mayor of Rockledge)*, H. E. Griggs *(Mayor of Cocoa)*, Dunn *(County Commissioner)*, Witter, Lewis, Knutson

1947 Fortenberry *(County Commissioner)*, Geiger *(Mayor of Rockledge)*, L. M. Carpenter *(County Commissioner)*, Griggs *(Mayor of Cocoa)*, Dunn *(County Commissioner)*, Lewis, Knutson

1948 Fortenberry *(County Commissioner)*, Geiger *(Mayor of Rockledge)*, Carpenter (County Commissioner), Griggs *(Mayor of Cocoa)*, Dunn *(County Commissioner)*, Lewis, Knutson

1949 Fortenberry *(County Commissioner)*, Geiger *(Mayor of Rockledge)*, Carpenter *(County Commissioner)*, Butt *(Mayor of Cocoa)*, Dunn *(County Commissioner)*, Lewis, Knutson

1950 Fortenberry *(County Commissioner)*, Butt, Lewis, Geiger *(Mayor of Rockledge)*, Knutson, Carpenter *(County Commissioner)*, Dunn *(County Commissioner)*

1951 D. S. "Dave" Nisbet *(County Commissioner)*, R. C. Burns, N. Argabrite, Carpenter *(County Commissioner)*, Dunn *(County Commissioner)*, Geiger *(Mayor of Rockledge)*, Butt *(Mayor of Cocoa)*

1952 Nisbet *(County Commissioner)*, Burns, Argabrite, Carpenter *(County Commissioner)*, Dunn *(County Commissioner)*, Geiger *(Mayor of Rockledge)*, Butt *(Mayor of Cocoa)*

1953 Nisbet *(County Commissioner)*, Burns, Argabrite, Carpenter *(County Commissioner)*, Dunn *(County Commissioner)*, Geiger *(Mayor of Rockledge)*, Butt *(Mayor of Cocoa)*

June 1953 Butt, Carpenter, Dunn, G. W. Laycock, Nisbet *(All appointed by Governor to constitute the new Board in accordance with new law, Chapter 28922 Law of Florida, Special Acts of 1953)*

1954 Butt, Carpenter, Dunn, Laycock, Nisbet

1955-1956 Kelly L. Brinson, Mayo Hill, Dunn, W. O. B. Chittenden, Laycock

1957-1958 Brinson, Chittenden, Dunn, Hill, and Laycock

1959 Brinson, Chittenden, John V. D'Albora, Dunn, Laycock *(Commissioner Chittenden resigned April 22, 1959, and Sion A. "Gus" Faulk, who had been appointed by Gov. Collins, was sworn in as a Port Commissioner. Mr. Dunn was elected Chairman.)*

1960 Brinson, Sion A. Faulk, D'Albora, Dunn, Laycock *(Roy Estridge appointed September 1960 to unexpired term of Laycock, deceased.)*

1961-1964 Brinson, Dunn, D'Albora, R. A. Cutter, Roderick S. McIver

1965 Brinson, Cutter, D'Albora, Dunn, McIver

1966 Brinson, Cutter, D'Albora, Dunn, McIver *(W. S. "Pappy" Austin appointed June, 1966 to unexpired term of A. A. Dunn, deceased.)*

1967-1968 W.S. Austin, Cutter, James H. Clendinen, McIver, Malcolm E. McLouth

1969-1972 Austin, William H. Clark, Clendinen, McIver, McLouth

1973 Austin, Clark, Clendinen, McIver, McLouth *(Commissioner Clark resigned effective August 31, 1973, to accept a position with his company in Seattle, Washington. Clyde Cowlin appointed to Board in December 1973 to fill vacancy left by Mr. Clark's resignation.)*

1974-1976 Austin, Clendinen, Cowlin, McIver, McLouth

1977 Austin, Clendinen, Wesley H. "Wes" Houser, McLouth, Nisbet

1978 Austin, Clendinen, Houser, McLouth, Nisbet

1979 Clendinen, Gilbert S. Goshorn, Houser, McLouth, Nisbet

1980 Clendinen, Goshorn, Houser, McLouth, Nisbet *(Resigned September 24, 1980, to assume office as Circuit Judge for the 18th Judicial Circuit Court of Florida.)*

1981-1982 M. M. "Buck" Buchanan, Clendinen, R. A. Cutter, Houser, McLouth

1983-1984 Jerry W. Allender, Buchanan, McLouth, Thomas L. Newbern, Nisbet

1985-1989 Allender, Buchanan, Sue Ford, McLouth, Newbern

1990 Allender, Buchanan, Ford, McLouth, Newbern *(Ralph J. Kennedy appointed November and December to unexpired term of Ford who resigned to seek another public office.)*

1991-1994 Allender, Buchanan, Kennedy, McLouth, Newbern

1995-1996 Raymond P. Sharkey, Buchanan, Donald Molitor, Kennedy, McLouth *(Rodney S. Ketcham appointed August 21, 1996 to complete McLouth's term.)*

1997-2002 Sharkey, Matheny, Molitor, Kennedy, Ketcham

2003 Sharkey, Joe D. Matheny, Tom Goodson, Kennedy, Ketcham